Fruity, a Little Bitter and Spicy

A Producer's Taste of the Global Olive Oil Industry

Simon Field

‘The International Olive Council (IOC) is committed to the integrated, sustainable development of world olive growing. It attempts to translate this commitment into tangible advancement for its member countries and, **most importantly, for the ordinary people who earn their livelihood from the produce of the olive tree**’. Extract from the International Olive Council Mission (www.internationaloliveoil.org)

This book is dedicated to the prosperity of those ‘ordinary people’ who earn their living from olive oil.

Ordinary:

not different or special or unexpected in any way; usual

Cambridge Dictionary.

(dictionary.cambridge.org/dictionary/english/ordinary)

‘Far from ordinary, the producers and purveyors of olive oil are special, unusual. Their toil supports the global olive oil industry.’

Simon Field, producer and founder ‘International Extra Virgin Olive Oil Savantes’.

St Arnaud, Victoria, Australia, March 2023

Simon Field

This book is based on personal experience, interaction and discussion with many people across the world who are, or have been, involved in the olive oil industry. Some of their comments have been related without identification, as when made they were not aware that this book would be written. The socio-economic and political commentary in the book is my considered opinion. Reference to institutions and associations has no purpose other than to provide a realistic contemporary framework for the narrative and ideas.

Written by Simon Field

1362 Dunolly Road
PO Box 104
St Arnaud, Victoria 3478
Australia

Telephone: +61 418 329 890

Email: simon@savantes.org

ISBN 978-0-6457327-0-2

About the Author.

Simon Field was born and spent his early years in Zimbabwe. He was brought up on his family's farm, Karimba, near Marondera, an hour east of the capital Harare.

He studied Natural Sciences at Trinity College, Cambridge University, and holds a Master of Arts. After graduation he travelled around the world on his own before returning to the farm. For the next ten years he farmed, married, and raised a family. In 1981 the family migrated to Australia and started a farming enterprise which they still own.

Following some involvement at the senior representative levels of farming organisations he was appointed the Executive Director of the Australian Institute of Agricultural Science, a position held for eight years.

In 1997 he resigned from the Institute and planted a 5,000 tree olive grove on the family farm. In 2001 he started International Extra Virgin Olive Oil Savantes, aiming to increase knowledge of extra virgin olive oil, initially in Australia, and then worldwide. Prior to the global pandemic Savantes organised regular events in 12 countries including the main olive oil producing and consuming regions. In 2019 Savantes coorganised the first International Extra Virgin Olive Oil Tasting Team Championship in Priego de Cordoba, Spain.

He has written handbooks on almost every aspect of olive oil and table olive production and marketing. He has presented numerous papers at conferences worldwide and written many articles on the production, politics, marketing and consumption of olive oil.

He frequently travels to olive growing and olive oil consuming regions and is a keen advocate for the advancement of the industry at all levels.

Contents

Prologue

Olive oil is the lifeblood of villages in the Mediterranean, Aegean and Adriatic. On this base is built an international trade which is demanding greater efficiency in production and distribution. On the margins are businesses built on the marketing of extra virgin olive oil comprising training, consulting, plant breeding, research, competitions, promotions, publications and cooking schools.

The book is a personal commentary from a producer who planted an olive grove at the turn of the century, developed related off-farm businesses, and progressed to being involved in international trading, promotion and professional events.

The stages of development are presented as they occurred over twenty-five years. The establishment of the grove and technical information are intermingled with the regional and global experience of operating in the olive oil industry.

It lays bare the mainstream industry, regional differences, parochialism, competition, burgeoning bureaucracy and fringe players who seek to profit from the primary product from olive groves, while the traditional producers languish.

Many of the actions of the industry belie the demands of excellence it imposes on its product: to exhibit balance, complexity, persistence and harmony. Remedial action is needed to deliver these positive attributes.

It is essential reading for anyone who contemplates being involved at any level in the international olive oil industry.

A First Taste

The romance of the olive grove and perceived benefits of consuming olive oil have captured the hearts and imagination of many over centuries. The reality of the labour required and limited financial returns have broken the hearts of just as many.

There is a constancy of production in the countries of the Mediterranean basin which are the traditional olive growing regions. Small grove ownership changes infrequently reflecting the closely held family businesses built around olive oil and agritourism. At the other end of the spectrum massive corporations and cooperatives aggregate these small properties into cohesive production and marketing units which attract finance from venture capital and large-scale investors.

The number of countries which are producing olive oil is increasing with expansion into Asia and the Southern Hemisphere – the so-called 'New World' olive oil producers. This development covers the same range of small producers to extensive corporate groves attracting many thousands of investors. These new olive industries tend to come in waves initiated by entrepreneurs with glossy prospectuses of the financial returns attracting investors ranging from individuals seeking new lifestyles to corporate managed investment schemes offered with tax minimisation benefits. Almost invariably these surges end within 15 to 20 years as the promised returns fall well short of expectation and the majority of the businesses are sold at a fraction of the original capitalised value. This rationalisation leaves a legacy of small, abandoned groves with a few larger enterprises continuing to trade efficiently and maintain a slightly elevated foundation for the next surge. The industry has no immunity from the boom-and-bust cycle which typifies agricultural production.

Whatever the reason for investing as a novice in this long-established industry, one can be assured that navigating a course through this highly complex global olive oil trade is challenging and exciting. There is a place for astute investors at every level. To find and maintain this place depends on acquiring the knowledge to make sensible decisions from establishment of the grove through to the markets targeted. Paradoxically, the decision should be the reverse of the commercial cycle, first choose the market then design the production enterprise to produce products which will be profitable in the chosen segment.

Unfortunately, many new enterprises take the approach that they will produce the product then worry about the sales. Abandoned groves are testament to the folly of this attitude.

The quest for knowledge will usually start with internet searches and participation in association events, conferences and courses. Experience reveals that almost all these events are held by those who have a vested interest in attracting participation and are sponsored by service suppliers who will not tolerate objective discussion on the viability of many aspects of the industry.

To get an objective assessment of the returns from olive oil production the potential investor must embark on a long-term direct involvement at every level of the industry. This is difficult to achieve prior to the initial investment, however, as will be demonstrated, it is possible once a foundation grove has been established to give first-hand knowledge of the production and marketing process.

In 1997, as a family, we established an olive grove on our farm in St Arnaud, Victoria, Australia. Many of the practices for good grove establishment were followed, others were not and 25 years later we are still paying for them. Some mistakes were of our own making, others were not and perpetrated by those we trusted in the early stages.

The Genesis of Savantes

We learned and instituted measures to check and double check information and products before committing to them. In parallel with the on-farm developments we have published handbooks on every aspect of olive oil production from grove establishment to marketing and selling. In response to the jingoistic catchcry that 'our extra virgin olive oil is the best in the world' we set about bringing together the most awarded oils from all over the world. To achieve this we worked with Judy Ridgway, an author and one of the world's most accomplished and independent olive oil tasters, to launch 'International Extra Virgin Olive Oil Savantes' in 2001. Through the Savantes programme we now organise tasting programmes in 12 countries and in 2019 held the first 'Extra Virgin Olive Oil Tasting Team World Cup' in Priego de Cordoba in Spain. In this event teams of three tasters from seven countries competed, with a producer team from Navarra in Spain becoming the first world champions.

The Savantes programme and associated activities connected us to some of the world's leading producers and decision-makers. We are fortunate to have a wide range of extra virgin olive oils supplied by producers for our events – our side of the contract is to be professional, independent, unbiased and objective. We do not receive any institutional support by way of grants and receive no encumbered sponsorship. We do not have a favourite olive oil, recognising the ebb and flow of quality and flavour profile affected by the seasons, we prefer to seek new flavours and new stories. We will never finish our quest to try extra virgin olive oils from every variety from every region. In our tasting sessions we mainly use olive oils from brands which consistently produce high quality products. Each year we send out a call for new products to be assessed for inclusion. The continued flow of olive oil is testament to our success in achieving these basic tenets.

To maintain this trust and currency of our Savantes programmes it is incumbent on us to keep up to date with the activities and trends along the entire worldwide supply chain. We achieve this by reading daily online newsletters from Spain, Italy, Greece, USA and scanning the internet for olive oil related articles. We do not necessarily accept the analysis and data provided by leading institutions and conduct our own research and analysis for presentations at Savantes programmes and conferences. Our independence and objectivity mean that we are often challenging the dictum of the day or the activities of vested interests.

These international activities are grounded by the return to the olive grove to harvest, prune and generally maintain our 5,000-tree grove. This brings us down to earth from the heady heights of international olive oil politics and trading. It gives time for assimilation and reflection on the situation for many small producers like us. It motivates us to share our experiences, observations and commentaries of many activities in the industry with those who cannot afford the time or do not have the means to garner the information required to make an informed decision.

We are producers in the new world and not constrained by the traditions of the long-time producing regions. We dare to question which makes us unpopular in some circles. However, we do know that our approach has motivated many to review and change their evaluation, marketing and selling of extra virgin olive oil.

Farmers in general are independent and suspicious of regulation and the bureaucracies which impose limits on their natural lifestyle. I confess to a degree of this which will be evident in some of the comments in this book. Where possible the assertions will be backed up with data, and where data is not available, perhaps the discussion will stimulate the generation of data.

It is a challenge to place a small olive grove in Australia in the world olive oil industry. This is a challenge any small producer must overcome. We hope our revelations and analysis will help 'ordinary people' acquire the knowledge which will give the resilience and dexterity to initiate, negotiate, influence and maintain profitable activities in the olive oil industry.

Choosing a Style

We decided to establish the olive enterprise after an eight-year stint managing the professional association for Australian agricultural scientists. A tertiary education in natural and agricultural science gave a head start with researching the olive project on the farm purchased in 1980. Wanting to return to farming as the primary source of income, we looked at various prospects including wool, a vineyard and wild flowers. It looked as if the wine industry was heading for a glut and the returns were unattractive even though contracts for any quantity of red wine grapes were readily available. The Victorian Pyrenees wine region, famous for its high quality red wines, is a few kilometres south of the farm. Having been involved in producing commodities on contract in the past we were wary of carrying all the capital development and the risks of production as well as being price takers. We wanted to produce a boutique product from the beginning to retail.

Australia was at the beginning of another surge in interest in olive products, especially olive oil. An entrepreneur had started an olive tree nursery and was widely promoting the prospects of lifestyle change and profits. The publicity attracted many professionals who were looking to invest in a pursuit which provided lifestyle, tax write-offs and a product which was surrounded by romance and passion. This cohort mainly invested in relatively small groves up to 20,000 trees. Another group, including farmers, established larger groves of 20,000 to 100,000 trees and then there were the Managed Investment Schemes which planted vast groves of many hundreds of thousands of trees.

Desk research helped assess the viability of olive oil production on an affordable scale. Critical to these calculations was the end price for the product. The prices promoted by the nurseries and others were around AU$7.00 per litre for extra virgin olive oil. Many looking to establish groves looked at the retail price for the few Australian boutique olive oils, which was AU$10-20 for a 500ml bottle, or AU$20-40 per litre, and worked on that. Others worked from estimated production costs and added a margin which would make the enterprise profitable.

Budgets based on these prices were flawed. Australia imported most of its olive oil of all grades from Europe. Realistically, the import price was the one which the nascent olive oil industry must compete with. This was confirmed by the one Australian brand which survived the previous surge and was still available in supermarkets at prices comparable with the higher end imported extra virgin olive oils.

The average price of imported extra virgin olive oils was $AU4.00 per litre, almost half the $AU7.00 generally promulgated by prospectuses and nurseries. The import parity price was used for our enterprise budgets. Using a wide range of sources to estimate establishment costs we worked out that the minimum size for a financially viable grove was 10,000 trees producing a conservative 4kg per tree, or 40 tonnes, of extra virgin olive oil a year.

We attended many conferences and seminars organised by the Australian Olive Association and talked to individuals to gather as much information as possible. Many of the events were sponsored by nurseries and equipment suppliers who had a vested interest in promoting the viability of the industry. The presentations mainly covered all activities relating to grove establishment and management and were light on the market and realistic trading conditions. The fact that Australia imported most of its requirements for olive oil which could be replaced by local production was offered as the major incentive for investing. The time lapse since the preceding surge in the olive industry meant that there were few who remembered previous attempts to replace imports.

It soon became apparent that a more independent delivery of information and scrutiny of projections was needed. Most of those providing expertise were Australian with newly acquired expertise, the few with international experience were tied to businesses whose primary objective was to expand the industry and profit from its rapid growth.

We registered the domain name olivebusiness.com and started to organise an annual Olive Business Conference to which were invited independent presenters, many from outside the industry who could give an objective assessment of its prospects. The conferences were sponsored by service suppliers, to be viable this was a necessity. However, the speakers were selected independently, and sponsorship gave no right to presentations. This is a philosophy which, often to our cost, we have maintained for the 25 years of activity in the industry.

The message delivered time and again by the successful agribusiness operatives from large food brands was to be cautious and realistic in budgeting. They reinforced the fact that we were entering a very well-established global industry and there was no rite of passage, the olive oil business being highly competitive.

One seminar which we organised to explore supermarket sales drew the wrath of the local Association President who was invited to attend. He described the conclusion of the seminar as unhelpful to the industry. Many producers aspired to have their packaged product available on the shelves of the major national supermarkets. To test the possibility of this we engaged with a former supermarket executive who had established an olive grove in his retirement. Together we presented a seminar which examined the opportunity for producers to access supermarkets. Participants were presented with a complex spreadsheet which detailed the costs and add-ons at every stage of the supermarket supply chain. It gave the volumes required, margins, promotional costs and many other supermarket imposts. The certification requirements, product guarantees, continuity of supply and penalties for non-compliance were all discussed.

The seminar was very valuable in our understanding of the market segment we should target, and it was not the supermarkets. Perhaps this revelation was the reason for the seminar being deemed as unhelpful as it blunted the common vision of supermarket shelves where local Australian brands replaced all the imports. This was unlikely as the supermarkets were reputed to have space for no more than five brands of olive oil, the existing imported brands were linked to long-time suppliers who also supplied a range of other products, and the price of locally produced olive oils was considerably higher. The shelves also contained several classifications of olive oil; extra virgin, extra light and olive oil. Only extra virgin was produced in Australia at this stage.

Defining the Product - Olive Oil

Olive oil is officially classified according to its quality and absence of defects. Extra virgin olive oil is the unadulterated and uncontaminated pressed juice of the olive. Virgin olive oil is the same except there may be some chemical specification and small flavour defects. This oil is rarely sold through mainstream retail, being used in foodservice or manufacturing. If oil does not meet these quality criteria it is deemed to be lampante olive oil and must be refined. The main flavour defects are caused through; rancidity, which is the result of oxidation, a mustiness caused by moulds in olives prior to processing, fermentation producing fustiness or winey-vinegary flavours, and finally the olives being frostbitten. There are many minor defects which will also lead to the oil being classified as lampante.

Refining of olive oil removes the odour, free fatty acids, colour and, in some cases, the fats which solidify first at a low temperature. The result is a colourless, odourless and tasteless olive oil sold as refined olive oil or blended back with a small quantity of extra virgin olive oil and sold as 'olive oil'. In some countries the refined oil can be sold as lite or extra lite olive oil.

Olive oil extracted from the residue left after the first extraction process is complete can be reprocessed through the centrifugal process to extract remnant oil. The final residue, known as pomace, can undergo a process of solvent extraction to remove every vestige of oil which is known as crude olive pomace oil. This is refined to olive pomace oil and while not recommended for human consumption can often be found in the kitchens of restaurants and hotels. Olive pomace oil can also be blended with a small portion of extra virgin olive oil to give it flavour, colour and aroma.

There is a place in the olive oil market for all the classifications. A complete industry needs the refining process to remove lampante oil from the market and provide a consistent, stable, and flavourless olive oil for many manufacturing applications. The highest prices are paid for extra virgin olive oil and from there in a descending scale to olive pomace oil. Producers can opt to produce extra virgin olive oil which comes from earlier harvested olives with a more robust flavour profile but a lower oil yield, or for later harvested, less flavour, higher yields of lower quality oil which may need refining. In some groves the olives are allowed to ripen to the point where they fall off the trees onto nets and the oil extracted, then refined. The producer calculates whether the reduced cost of harvesting and the substantially higher oil yields from this refined oil gives better returns than the higher quality extra virgin olive oil which requires more costly inputs. In addition to harvesting, these inputs can include expensive fungicides and pesticides to limit attack from fungal disease such as anthracnose or pests such as olive fly. The longer the olives stay on the tree the more likely they will be affected by insects, diseases and frost. Refining removes from the oil the off tastes and odours caused by these pestilences.

It is common practice in the industry amongst the producers of extra virgin olive oil and their representatives to denigrate or talk down refined olive oil. The motivation is probably to shift the users of refined olive oil and other vegetable oils to using extra virgin olive, thereby increasing the market for their product.

This is a short-sighted approach for several reasons. Not everybody likes the strong bitter and peppery flavours of extra virgin olive oil despite the constant promotion of the health benefits of intensely flavoured oils. Extra virgin olive oil costs much more than refined olive oil, blends of olive oils, and other vegetable oils and many consumers cannot afford it. For some cooking and manufacturing processes a consistent flavourless olive oil is required. Refined olive oil has a higher smoke point than extra virgin olive oil and is more appropriate for cooking and manufacturing processes at higher temperature. Finally, if all current consumers of refined olive switched to extra virgin olive oil there simply would not be enough as world production of this classification is less than 50% of all olive oil consumed.

The socio-economic implications of this approach must be considered. There are many producers who cannot produce extra virgin olive and make a reasonable living from producing lampante oil for refining. The environment and weather sometimes preclude the production of extra virgin olive oil despite the best managerial efforts of the farmer.

This is an example of information which those promoting a new industry will not make available and stresses the importance of thorough research.

Establishing the Grove

Having ascertained that our olive project was viable if we sold products through the boutique or foodservice channels, we set about the process of establishing the grove. Important in the budget was that we did the work ourselves and did not incur the substantial cost and risk of employing labour or contractors.

The most important consideration when establishing or buying an olive grove is location. Olive trees have the reputation of being very hardy and growing anywhere naturally. This is generally true except in extreme environments such as very low temperatures or tropical heat and high rainfall. The trees may grow, but the question is are they productive? A simple approach to determine whether the location is right is to look around for existing groves and try to find out how productive they are.

Olive trees around the world have thrived in Mediterranean-like climates with hot dry summers and cold winters with spring rainfall. Summer rainfall in the tropics and sub-tropics will promote excessive vegetative growth and little fruit production. The humid conditions also encourage the growth of fungal diseases which attack the roots, leaves and fruit. Insect infestation may also be more of a problem in warmer humid climates.

In very cold climates the tree growth may be stunted and with the shorter ripening season the fruit may not achieve acceptable yields of oil. A question at a seminar held in Wellington in New Zealand highlights this problem. 'Where can I buy trees which produce black olives', a participant asked. The producer had established a grove and observed that the fruit did not ripen to black, a function of the seasonal conditions. The question also revealed a lack of knowledge of the simplest horticultural interaction of the olive tree with the environment. New Zealand produces some excellent extra virgin olive oil; however, the quantities are small and the prices of the product relatively high.

There is a range of options for entry into olive growing; planting a grove on an existing landholding, purchasing undeveloped land or purchasing an existing grove. Assuming the climate is conducive to growing olives for olive oil there are some agronomic and market considerations to be covered.

The important agronomic factors are the type of soil, acidity, drainage and availability of water. Generally, the soil should be well drained and the aspect of the grove giving maximum sunlight. Waterlogging is a major problem for olive trees giving rise to root diseases which can severely affect growth and, in some cases, kill many trees. Olives will grow in areas of relatively low rainfall but need irrigated water to maximise fruit production and consequently high yields of olive oil. An extreme example of the selection of location are groves in Peru which have been established in a desert near an oasis fed from the surrounding mountains. This gives total control of water application with the added benefit that the pest population in the desert is virtually non-existent, making pest management easier.

The simplest way to check the soil conditions is to invest a small amount of money to engage a soil scientist to conduct a comprehensive soil survey. This will give a profile of the soil, drainage, presence of rock and soil nutrients. You may well find, as we did, that the site selected was not appropriate because of a layer of red clay soil which resulted in poor drainage. The location was moved to an area of better drained soil. Even then we found that in one small area there was a layer of rock close to the surface which affected drainage and resulted in waterlogging and trees dying. Only when the surrounding trees were mature and mitigating the waterlogging were we able to establish trees in this small area.

Checking the agronomic conditions is no less important when buying an existing grove. Looking at the trees will give an idea of the health of the soil, with dieback being evidence of root disease caused by waterlogging. Always walk through the entire grove as the trees on the outside may well be healthier and bear more fruit than those inside where there is more competition from adjacent trees. Ask for any aerial photographs of the grove which will show any variations in the growth of the trees and use Google Earth or a drone to inspect the grove from above and check the surrounding areas for any aberrations. Dead trees in an adjacent grove may indicate a local problem. There are many possible reasons for the sale of a grove, sometimes the incidence of disease, poor growth and productivity may result in the owners deciding to move on. The reason should be explored to ensure that the local growing conditions are not the problem. The decision to sell may be brought on by low prices for the product, varieties which have problems, change of life of the owners, family disagreements or insolvency. The intending purchaser should pursue the reason until a satisfactory answer is provided. The decision then becomes whether any issues with the horticultural aspects of the grove can be rectified for a reasonable cost. If there are major problems, it is probably wiser to walk away and look for another option.

Marketing considerations are extremely important. At this stage of planning the market segment that your product will target should have been determined. The volume of product the market can absorb at a given price point should be in your budget. This can range from very small production which will be sold through farmers' markets or online, to larger volumes sold through retail or the 'Horeca' food service channel. Horeca is an acronym for Hotel, Restaurant and Catering. When estimating the turnover of a market be wary of the 'it walks off the shelf' response from a retailer. Nothing walks off the shelf and the actual volumes sold can be a fraction of your expectation.

The simplest way to sell your product is as raw fruit. It may the simplest, but it is the least profitable. From there the process of preparing your olive oil product for sale becomes increasingly complex with each stage – harvesting, extraction, storage, bottling, labelling, compliance, distribution, billing, credit control, promotion and product recall.

You have the option of having your olives processed to oil by a 'toll' or contract processor. Proximity to toll processors who are adept millers will reduce the time between harvesting and processing. Try to be close enough to more than one mill so you have options if processing charges increase, or machinery breaks down. Other considerations are; time 'slots' for processing at harvesting time convenient for your grove, cleanliness of the mill, trust that you are getting your product and not someone else's, and there is no contamination. It is best to observe the processing of your olives. Make sure you have an agreement with the miller to cover any contamination, adulteration or any other eventuality you can think of.

Another option is to install your own extraction plant. This is a large capital expense at start-up so you should be cautious. Efficient olive oil extraction takes experience and good machinery. It is no coincidence that the same millers around the world consistently produce extra virgin olive oils which win the most prestigious awards. Knowledge of the different nuances of each variety comes with experience, as does the impact on processing of olives with high water content in wet seasons, and very low moisture in droughts.

We decided to have our olives toll processed to start with while we worked out yields and the cost-effectiveness of processing ourselves. We have never installed an olive oil processing plant for reasons revealed later.

Proximity to mills and markets in which you have confidence is important. You may decide to deliver your products direct to retail or Horeca, or use a distributor, or both. You can also sell online. If you sell through a third party ensure that you do not undercut their price with your direct sales, this makes them upset. It is wise not to try to dictate the price for which they sell your product, this will also upset them. Refrain from putting a recommended retail price on the label or your website.

The distribution system you choose is important for transport and frequency of delivery, for example, Horeca customers do not have much storage space and little control over volumes consumed. They will suddenly find they are short of your product and telephone for a delivery – now. You must deliver or someone else will. No matter how hard you try to put a system in place which anticipates their requirements it eventually unravels with you dashing off again to deliver a small quantity of product. This ad hoc delivery system is expensive and time consuming if you live far out of town.

In summary, for location of your olive grove you must optimise the growing conditions such as soil, weather and water supply. Choose a location which has these requirements and access to services such as processing, bottling and distribution. Once these are optimised the price of the property comes into consideration and your decision will be a balance of location and the price of the land.

There are other factors which are less important but warrant research. Many regional and local administrations have regulations which may affect your production process; noise levels, food safety regulations, building compliance, use of pesticides and herbicides, control of run-off, disposal of processing waste, and burning prunings are some to be investigated. We found that there was an indigenous heritage overlay placed on part of our property 20 years after we purchased it, and we didn't know that it had been enacted. The legal proceedings to have our processing plant plans approved and the site cleared of cultural artefacts would have added considerable cost to the processing facility.

Talk to local administrators, neighbours, olive oil enterprises, distributors, consumers and anyone else whom you can think of before committing to buying the chosen property. Then with your budget you are set to establish or buy your dream olive grove and start your adventure in an exciting global olive oil industry.

Selecting The Flavour

Diligently following these basic procedures necessary to ensure we have a sound foundation for the olive enterprise leads to ownership of the land with the soil survey complete. The olive grove area is fenced off and the time has come to decide on the trees. Varieties dictate the flavour of the olive oil along with a range of other managerial factors. Varieties and spacing are the main considerations. The two are interconnected in modern groves where super high-density plantings with hedge-like tree spacing and trellising are only suitable for certain varieties. There are a few which are part-proven in high-density and many more that are being bred to suit this style of production. The former are koroneiki, arbequina, arbosana and FS17, with some of the newer ones being arroniz, tosca and sikitita. A word of warning here, there are many names for some of these varieties, for example FS17 is also known as favalosa. There are also many clones of each variety which show different characteristics.

When you have selected and planted your varieties you are stuck with them at least until they can manifest their productivity, ease of management, and disease resistance. If you get it wrong, it is an expensive mistake necessitating either top grafting with another variety or the replacement of the unproductive varieties.

At the time we were selecting our varieties there was a very aggressive marketing campaign to sell a new variety from Israel – barnea. Newly established nurseries bought a licence to sell this variety and it was planted in the new world groves – Australia, New Zealand and in South America. Some very large groves were established and many of them are now pulling out the mature trees and replacing them with proven varieties. The promotion of barnea was glowing, a vigorous variety with early production producing a high percentage of high quality olive oil. Added to all this, it was dual-purpose, good for producing table olives as well. We resisted planting the variety and bought a few to place in mother pollinator rows to see how they performed. This is a good way to test trees which are unproven. The barnea trees outgrew all the other seven varieties in the same row and needed twice as much pruning. The yield was as good as the other established varieties and the disease and drought resistance acceptable. The olive oil was of reasonable quality with distinct fruity flavours, but even here there was a catch. The International Olive Council (IOC) has a published set of Trade Standard specifications which provide limits for some of the chemical markers in olive oil which indicate the possibility of adulteration with refined olive oil or seed oils. One of these markers is the level of campesterol. Barnea was found to have out of specification levels of campesterol if grown in certain conditions. This meant that the oil could not be sold as olive oil unless blended with another olive oil low in campesterol, thereby bringing the blend within the specified levels. The trouble was that one very large Managed Investment Grove in Australia planted over 60% of its grove to barnea and did not have enough oil from other varieties for blending.

An expensive campaign ensued where the Australian growers' association tried to change the international specifications, with limited success. The barnea trees are now being removed at great expense and replaced. Ironically, the company which owned the nursery enterprise which supplied many of the barnea trees ended up acquiring the large grove when it was liquidated and inherited the trees they had sold. Some kind of karma? Credit to them, the nursery ceased selling the variety and made the following observation on its website, 'Unfortunately many growers in Australia who planted trees in the last eight years purchased and planted trees that were not suitable or up to standard. Only now are they realising the extent of their problems. It is cheaper and easier to do it right the first time'. Mea culpa? Lesson learned and sage words which are little consolation to those to whom they sold the trees. Be careful if you are buying unproven varieties to be planted in yet unproven and independently endorsed production systems. New varieties may perform well in some regions and not others due different soils and climate. Check that the production system you are about to adopt has been objectively assessed to be viable in the relevant growing conditions by an organisation which is independent from the nurseries and sellers of the systems with associated equipment.

In the prospectuses and online information used to select the varieties we would plant there were many data on expected oil yields, mainly from European groves. Experience shows that this information is not necessarily transferable to different regions and growing conditions. This is not surprising, as many of the varieties have developed in the microclimates around villages where the different olives have grown for centuries. If you are in a region where olives for oil are already grown, you should be able to get useful data from the grove owners. Questions should include; the nurseries where the seedlings were purchased, any indications of disease resistance or predisposition to infection, drought and frost resistance, flowering and ripening times, as well as oil yield and quality.

When choosing varieties, it is best to plant a mixture to minimise the risk of failure. If you manage and provide the labour for your harvesting it is also a good idea to have those which flower, pollinate and ripen sequentially. Again, it spreads the risk of events such as a late frost decimating flowers throughout the grove if all the trees are flowering at once. Mixed species extends the period of pollination and the olives ripening at different times allows you to spread the work of harvest over weeks or months. Of course, if you need to harvest during a short period you can wait for a range of ripeness and harvest everything at once, effectively blending at the harvest.

Another point to note when buying trees is whether they are grafted or not. It is common practice to graft olive trees using rootstock which is vigorous to support a productive variety. Rootstock of local, sometimes wild, olive trees often has resistance to soilborne diseases and is acclimatised to the growing conditions, be they wet or dry. Check which rootstock has been used. Nurseries may find that a particular variety is not selling, and a faster return will be realised if they graft more popular trees onto the rootstock. Be wary of this grafting brought about through expediency rather than horticultural wisdom.

Frost resistance is an important characteristic of some olive varieties and it is possible to map the variation in elevation of the grove to highlight sheltered areas prone to low temperatures with frost. This can be done at the same time as mapping the different soil types. Frost resistant and early ripening trees can be planted where the frost is a risk with the later ripening trees on more elevated ground where damage is less likely.

Observation in our grove where varieties are planted in blocks shows that different varieties are more prone to disease than others. The grove is organic, and no pesticide, fungicide or herbicide has been used. The only pest control we used at one stage was white mineral oil to control scale. We discontinued this after 10 years for reasons which will be explained when organic production is discussed in more detail.

If you have an established grove there is the option of propagating your own trees. Careful observation and records will help select trees that are frost, drought and more disease resistant, and of course consistently produce good yields of fruit with a high percentage of good quality oil. Cuttings are taken from these and propagated giving you acclimatised trees with a proven production record. One third of our grove is populated with trees we propagated ourselves with the added benefit that they are also organically raised and do not know what a herbicide or pesticide is. Propagating olive trees is not difficult. If your grove trees are not the varieties you want, you have the option of top-grafting cuttings from the varieties you desire. There are many ways of top grafting depending on the maturity of the trees.

A practice which is useful when contemplating any changes is to try it with a few trees before taking the plunge and doing the whole lot which can be risky. This applies to nutrient application, pruning, new varieties, top grafting and any other untried management.

An excellent example of the use of grafting involves the African Olive, Olea africana and the European Olive, Olea europaea. The former originates from Asia Minor and genetic analysis suggests that it is the precursor of the olive we know so well which populates the Mediterranean basin. The European olive has been bred to produce fruit which has a high level of olive oil or is suitable for processing as table fruit. The African olive has evolved without selective breeding and can be found spread naturally all over Asia and Africa. It is hardy with small fruit with a large pit and little flesh, hence little olive oil. When the migrants from the Mediterranean arrived in the South African Cape of Good Hope, they found that the olive trees which they brought from Europe and planted did not thrive. They grafted the cuttings onto rootstock of the indigenous African olive and the trees were hardier and more productive. Now it is common practice in Southern Africa and Asia Minor to graft the ancient and modern olives.

Despite its low oil content, the African olive holds a special place in the culture of the black people of Africa where it is used for traditional ceremonies and natural medicines. The wood is extremely hard and was used for crafting weapons such as spears and knobkerries, as well as making decorative ornaments and beads.

On top of all these horticultural aspects of variety selection there is the profile of the product they produce, olive oil. The order the aspects have been dealt with is intentional, first you need to have productive trees to be profitable, then you need the range of flavours of olive oil to differentiate your product.

We will deal with many aspects of the flavours of olive oil in detail later. Here we will list the options you have which are dictated by the market in general and information you can access without being an expert taster.

Factors Affecting Flavour

Approximately 40 percent of the world's olive oil comes from Spain. Thirty percent of the Spanish oils come from the variety picual. We can deduce from this that picual is used in many blends coming out of the two largest producers and exporters of olive oil, Spain and Italy. Olive oil from ripe picual has a very distinctive taste and an expert taster will detect it in many supermarket extra virgin olive oils, whether they have Spanish or Italian brand names. New rules state that the origin of the oils must be listed on the label so one can check if there is Spanish oil in the blend. The brand name means little these days as the major brands are owned by huge corporations and the Italian or Spanish name is just that and cannot be assumed to indicate the country of origin of the contents. With this predominance of picual in mainstream blends, it can be argued that many consumers worldwide are used to the taste and aroma of picual oil, and it is easier to sell something they are used to than invest in a product which is new to the market. Consider this variety which has proved to grow well in a range of environments. One caveat is that if the moisture content of the olive at harvesting is high, it is hard to extract the oil from the picual fruit.

There are many factors other than variety which have an impact on the flavour profile of extra virgin olive oil. Early harvesting of green olives will tend to give you a stronger tasting or more robust oil and, as ripening progresses from green to black, the oil content increases and the intensity of the flavour declines. A late harvested oil will have a more delicate flavour. The components in extra virgin olive oil which impart the flavour are the biophenols, sometimes known as polyphenols, which are also antioxidants. These help delay oxidisation of stored olive oil which progresses with time and ultimately renders the oil rancid.

There is a matrix of flavour profiles affected by the variety and harvest timing which impact on the shelf-life and consumer preference. Add to these that polyphenols are water soluble, so in a wet year or with irrigation the levels in the oil will be lower and the flavour diluted.

The extraction method is also important with some processes involving washing and added water which again dilutes the flavour components. Modern olive oil extraction involves three main processes – crushing, mixing and centrifugation. The olives are delivered, washed and crushed into a paste in a hammer mill. The paste is pumped into a malaxer or mixing cylinder where a spiral paddle slowly mixes the paste so the olive oil droplets can aggregate before the paste is pumped into the centrifuge or decanter. The fast-spinning centrifuge separates the oil which is run off into a storage tank while the vegetable water and solid matter or pomace go separate ways. The oil is often put through other filtering processes to remove remnant water and solids before being stored in stainless steel tanks. The old and traditional method of crushing the olives with rotating stones and packing the paste in mats in a hydraulic press has mostly been superseded by the modern centrifugal extraction.

Yes, it is very complicated and there are some decisions you can make on varieties which will give you a number of options for the flavour profile of your oil and the market you are targeting.

If you are purchasing an existing grove, your options are limited in that the varieties are already there. First you need to identify the varieties which in some of the older established groves may be difficult, especially when the plantings have been done in haphazard way over many decades or centuries. A good start is to talk to the previous owners and the locals to get an idea of whether the trees are local varieties or from another region. For example, in Italy many of the towns and villages have very localised varieties which suit the environment and have grown with the cuisine of the region. The taggiasca variety is an example of this in the Ligurian region of Italy. The variety is not grown in any other part of the world except in small experimental pockets. The oil is super delicate with subtle aromas and tastes well suited to the fish-based cuisine of the region. The low antioxidant level means the oils have a short shelf-life even if early harvested. For this reason, the oil is rarely available in export markets and even then, some brands have the bottles wrapped in gold or silver foil to limit the deterioration caused by another enemy of olive oil – light.

A lovely taggiasca oil was brought to one of our tastings in Sevilla by a family from Canada who produced olive oil on their small grove in Liguria. It was presented in a simple white ceramic container with a cork seal. To this day I remember the exquisite aroma of pure vanilla which blossomed when the bottle was opened. The aroma carried through to the palate, which is not always the case. Apart from being an example of the flavour expression of a variety, this oil serves to show that from a small grove an exclusive, differentiated and distinctive product can be produced which virtually sells itself at a good return. The trick is to repeat this profile each year which is not easy with the vagaries of the weather, pestilence and everything else that tests the mettle of the farmer.

However attractive this micro-production may be, I do not suggest you plant taggiasca in a new grove outside Liguria, there is a reason it is not found elsewhere, and the chances of success are small. If you do want to dabble in this sort of variety, plant a small number of trees as an experiment.

Back to sorting out which trees you have in your newly acquired grove. After you have exhausted local sources of information you can search the internet for evidence of the foliage and the shape of the fruit. You may find that in the grove there are trees with a variety of leaf and fruit shapes, and even the way the fruit hangs from the branches may help. The progressive colour changes when the fruit ripens may add some information which will help with identification. You can also search the 'World Catalogue of Olive Varieties' published by the International Olive Council. It may be a little outdated but contains most of the traditional varieties from all regions with excellent pictures of morphological characters such as leaf and fruit shape which will help with identification.

There are some institutions in the main producing regions which can analyse the DNA of the olive leaves and fruit and compare it to the bank of genetic material they hold for varietal identification. This can be used as a last resort, but the cost may preclude this option.

Why is identification important? Because it gives you greater flexibility right through your management of the tree to harvest timing and blending the final product. The more flexibility the easier it is to adapt to changing supplies of labour, variable seasons and meeting the demands of the market with a more differentiated product.

A spreadsheet with the layout of the grove and each tree is a useful tool. Colour codes can identify the different varieties and worksheets can be devoted to trees afflicted by particular diseases or any other event worthy of recording. Such a worksheet helped identify the spread of a fungal disease through our grove. It became clear that it spread over a few years from a particular group of trees with fungal spores vectored on the prevailing wind. This type of information is of great value when deciding on tactics to reduce infection in an organic grove. In one extreme case a new producer who established a grove as a lifestyle choice to give a break from his information technology business barcoded each tree with a programme to record relevant data. A useful tool for disease recording and other horticultural management, however of little use for its original intention which was to record yield by tree which was impractical during the rush of mechanical harvesting. It may work for hand harvesting, the question being as to what to do with the data. Seasoned farmers will note patterns and trends and act accordingly. The bar coding is a nice idea for tree identification in a haphazardly planted grove and spreadsheets are also useful in planning the distribution of varieties in a new grove.

Selecting Varieties from Regions

It is recommended that for flexibility you select varieties that will grow in your environment which reflect the ethnic preferences of the market. The major users of olive oil are the Greeks, Italians and Spanish. It is wise to cover varieties from these countries in your plantings to give the opportunity to target particular taste preferences manifest in ethnic cuisine which has now penetrated all countries of the world. The ubiquitous Greek variety is koroneiki which produces a delicate to medium intensity olive oil suitable for cuisine including fish as well as more intense flavoured cooking. The choice of varieties in Italy is more diverse with each region having a 'variety' profile which was unique before the new world and other regions started planting them. The famed Tuscan varieties are frantoio, leccino and moraiolo with pendolino used as a pollinator. The reputation of Tuscan production outstrips its volume which is around 4% of total Italian production. The flavour of the oils from these varieties is popular and suits all cuisine. Leccino goes black early and is the first to ripen, although it should not be judged by the colour of its skin. The blackness is not an indication of ripeness measured by the oil accumulation. Frantoio seems to be a fickle variety which yields well in some areas and not others. In Australia there is a variety called corregiolo which originates from Italy, is related to frantoio, has grown in Australia for a long time and has become acclimatised. It is a high yielder producing a high percentage of oil with an excellent flavour profile. In Australia this may be a better prospect than frantoio.

Beware the traps of taking a variety which is related to another because the one you want is not available. Nevadillo blanco is a Spanish variety related to picual. However, in our grove it is a poor yielder and the oil has a very distinctive and pungent 'cat' aroma. The nursery recommended this as an alternative to picual which was sold out. In retrospect we were naïve to accept their recommendation. We only planted a few so the financial cost is not great. The trees are beautiful so if you are looking for an ornamental tree for the garden plant nevadillo blanco, not for the grove. Our flexible approach has helped us find a use for the nevadillo fruit as small table olives. The fruit is generally very bitter and takes two years to ferment and prepare for the bitter-averse consumer. The table olive flavour is different from other varieties and the financial return is almost five times more than selling the oil.

Heading further south in Italy to Puglia which produces 40% of Italy's oil we find the variety coratina. Producing a more robust oil this variety has proved adaptable to many regions and along with the Tuscan quartet is worth considering. There are other varieties in Puglia which make excellent oil such as peranzana and ogliarola, however they are not grown in large numbers in other regions or countries. Beyond the toe of the Italian 'boot' in Sicily, a variety that has been grown in South Africa and other parts of the new world is nocellara del belice. Be careful, there are a number of nocellaras emanating from different regions in Italy and more than one in Sicily. The fruit of nocellara del belice produces excellent flavoured oil as well as being the green table olive which has become so well-known worldwide. Biancolilla and cerasuolo are other varieties found in the excellent blends coming from Sicily, again they are not common outside the region.

Summarising Italian varieties which have proven they can be grown in a range of environments and be used to produce Italian style oils it is suggested you look at frantoio, leccino, pendolino as a pollinator, coratina and nocellara del belice. As a bonus, frantoio and leccino make an excellent small table olive – green, turning colour or black – and nocellara del belice is excellent for natural fermentation as a green table olive or through treatment with lye as the classic Sicilian Castelvetrano style bright green table olive.

And on to Spain where vast acreages of olives cover the land to the horizon and produce copious amounts of extra virgin olive oil of all intensities and diverse flavours. The main varieties which are evident in plantings in new regions are picual from Andalucia which has already been mentioned, arbequina which originates from the north in Catalunya, hojiblanca which comes from a pocket around Priego de Cordoba and manzanilla which doubles as a table olive. Arbequina tends to produce a delicate to medium intensity oil while hojiblanca produces a robust highly aromatic oil which does well in many Iberian and international competitions. Spanish varietal oils tend to be more bitter than other Mediterranean regions and manzanilla extra virgin olive oil is amongst the most bitter. Two other Spanish varieties of note amongst the many regional oils are cornicabra from the Castilla la Mancha region and picuda from Cordoba. Neither of these are extensively cultivated outside these regions.

To summarise Spanish varieties worth assessing; picual and arbequina are extensively planted and hojiblanca produces outstanding olive oils with very attractive flavour profiles, it is often blended with about five per cent of picuda to give it complexity, balance and harmony.

Varieties in other countries which are worth looking at are picholine and l'aglandau from France and cobrancosa from Portugal. Mission is a variety found in South Africa and California which is essentially a table olive now used for oil production. The mother stock originates from Spain and the trees were taken to California by the missionaries, hence the name mission. The polyphenol level is relatively low giving a sweeter less robust oil with a relatively short shelf-life. Oil yields are reasonable so it can be used as a blending oil. However, groves filled with table olive varieties should be used for table olives.

Frequently one sees that a table olive variety such as kalamata, ascolana, mission, cerignola, sevillano, verdale and others win gold medals in extra virgin olive oil competitions. Often these varieties produce attractive flavoursome oils, however, the oil yields are generally half of the yields from olives grown for oil production and these varieties should not be planted with the expectation of commercial oil yields.

Regions tend to continue to propagate the varieties which are proven in their environment and fit in with the current expectation of flavours for the local cuisine and established export markets. Increasingly, especially in Spain, varieties from other countries are being planted in new groves. Frantoio and koroneiki are being planted in Navarra and Andalucia in Spain, arbequina is being planted in Greece. One would expect the flavour profiles of oils from these plantings in new regions to be similar to oils in the regions of origin.

However, Spanish grown frantoio and koroneiki with the regional management, harvesting and processing methods result in Spanish style oils which are more robust and sharper than the more mellow Italian and Greek versions. There are some common flavour characteristics, but the overall style of the oil differs.

In the new world plantings, Australasia, South Africa, South America, California, China, India, Pakistan and Japan investors have taken the opportunity to plant a mixture of the recognised producing varieties. This is commercially sensible as the monovarietal oils and blends can be produced to meet the needs of any buyer or market.

A new development promulgated by large corporations involved in selling production systems worldwide is the high-density and super high-density olive groves. These will be dealt with from a grove design perspective in the next chapter. Not all olive varieties are compatible with high-density planting, resulting in a new wave of plant breeding and selection to find varieties which perform well in these systems. When you see a range of monovarietal oils which come from the arbequina, arbosana and koroneiki varieties you can bet it is a high or super high-density grove. Oliana, arbosana, lecciana and sikitita are also planted in high-density. Generally, these varieties yield extra virgin olive oils with relatively low polyphenol levels which may not meet the minimum stipulated by some jurisdictions to claim the health benefits attributed to the product. To overcome this perceived deficiency, plant breeders for these high-density configurations are attempting to breed arbequina with a higher level of polyphenols. Sikitita is the result of cross-breeding arbequina and picual to achieve the same end. Oliana has been developed from arbequina and arbosana and lecciana is also a new addition to the super high-density varietal catalogues. No doubt other varieties will be the subject of similar breeding and selection programmes. This development is given much publicity and the information will be reviewed when we discuss grove layout and all the related management issues. Suffice it to say here that if you are going for high-density planting don't just select any variety and plant it like a hedge!

Production

This is not intended to be a technical guide giving detailed advice on grove management. Such advice is available from many associations, government departments and online. Here we will give you a framework within which you can make management decisions.

Two critical decisions to be made early in your planning which have a continuing effect on your management are whether to make your grove organic and what tree layout and density you will plant.

Organic or Not?

Organic certification is very prescriptive, starting with the source of your trees which must have been organically propagated. From there the organic mantra dictates how you do virtually everything in the grove and post-harvest handling. If you are going down the organic road it is best to make the decision early and design the grove and facilities accordingly. You will be required to sample and analyse the soil from specified areas in the grove to determine the chemical profile and evidence of any residues from inorganic fertiliser, bactericides, fungicides, herbicides and pesticides. Finding out the prior history of application of these substances will help define the organic profile of the grove area.

Buffer zones must be established between adjacent properties where chemicals may be applied. Water run-off should be assessed to ensure that contamination of groundwater from the surrounding area is unlikely. The organic certifying body will provide guidelines which you should study before making major decisions on layout and grove management.

Selecting the most appropriate organic certifying body will help with the continuing compliance and costs. There are innumerable fees for inspections, soil and tissue testing for residues, as well as the fee for membership of the accrediting body. Many of the fees are time-based with travel costs for inspections passed on in the bill so it is wise to consider the location and cost of inspectors as well. If you intend to process your olives, the facility will need to comply with organic specifications along with bottling facilities, packaging and labelling. Your inputs must be organic – all of them. There is a lot of additional management and cost to producing a certified organic product. You must satisfy yourself that the premium obtained at wholesale or retail for the organic status will at least lead to recovery of these costs.

Our grove is organic and has been for the full 25 years since establishment. We had to go through a three-year probationary period at the beginning to rid the grove of any previously applied chemicals and to quarantine the trees which we bought from the nursery – there were no organic nurseries which could supply the quantity and varieties we needed. If you decide to go organic, don't let the availability of varieties from the organic nurseries dictate the varieties you plant, get the varieties from non-organic nurseries and quarantine them for the required period before planting. The quarantine period and conditions vary with certifying agencies, at least the trees are still growing while they wait out the specified period.

After 12 years we dropped the organic certification for multiple reasons, the main one being that the premium paid for our products was not covering the burgeoning cost of organic certification fees and the levies which the agency demanded as a percentage of sales. There were disputes over the use of some substances which were allowed in processing of other foodstuffs and not for table olives. To this day we have not used chemicals on the grove and do not apply inorganic fertiliser. We rely on natural methods of fertilisation from clover and the substantial mob of kangaroos which have made the grove their preferred location. They provide natural fertiliser and keep the grass and weeds down, and being soft-footed, do not compact the soil as cloven-hoofed animals, such as sheep, do. We are farmers without a tractor which, along with our organic and 'green' philosophy manifest in the farm being a wildlife sanctuary, makes the local farmers shake their heads in disapproval and earns us the label of tree-huggers!

Over the years we have seen many natural controls come back into the grove and slowly the pest population has become an insect population. The birds have multiplied and help with insect balance. An example is the infestation of the trees with the circulio beetle which devours the foliage leaving serrated edges to the leaves. Canny creatures, they live in the soil at the base of the trees, coming out to feed at night climbing the trunk then heading back to their safe haven in the soil before the sun rises. To catch them on their nightly forays we put a band of raw wool around the trunk and the weevil-like beetles got caught up in the fibre. We have small cohorts of the insect-eating black choughs roaming the grove. Our interest in pop music led us to name them the Hilltop Hoods as they traverse the grove in their group of six or seven. Another group is known as the Blackstreet Boys and the two bands of choughs often clash over feeding grounds. The birds learned that there was a feast to be had each morning from the wool and ate the insects while dismantling the wool bands making a mess around the trees. They soon worked out that the insects inhabited the soil around the base of the trees and now go direct to dig them out, saving the trees, and us the labour of constantly replacing the wool bands.

We observe that the trees have also started to become more resistant to some of the most pervasive fungal diseases such as sooty mould and associated scale insects which cover the trees in a black powdery layer severely affecting their productivity. Recently we have noticed a substantial increase in the ladybird population which predate on scale and the disappearance of the ants which milk the scale for honeydew. It seems the grove is reaching its own equilibrium for disease control without intervention with human-made chemicals. This development has implications for the high-density groves which we will now explore.

The Olive Tree's Natural Defence System

The polyphenols in olive oil emanating from the olive fruit are not there to please the human palate and give advertisers the opportunity to promote the health benefits of consuming extra virgin olive oil, they are the defence mechanism for the fruit. The same applies to the antioxidants much vaunted in the medicinal extract from olive leaves which protect the leaves from fungal and insect attack. The polyphenols acting as antioxidants protect our health and that of the olive tree.

It is logical that if we treat all the diseases and pests of olive trees with artificial means such as pesticides and fungicides, we are reducing the requirement for the tree to develop its own resistance. Just as humans in sanitised or highly medicated environments do not develop antibodies and when exposed to less sanitary or non-medicated situations, they are more prone to affliction. In applying copious amounts of pesticides and fungicides to our groves we are selecting against naturally disease resistant trees and destroying the natural predators which control disease and infestations. We see this in the grove, varieties like arbequina and kalamata which have low levels of polyphenols are more prone to fungal attack than the picual and manzanilla trees which have high polyphenol levels. Arbequina, in particular, is blackened by the ever-present sooty mould which coats the branches and leaves, severely limiting photosynthesis.

The proximity of other olive groves or concentrations of other fruit trees or plants will be a potential host or incubator for disease. Buffer zones may act as a physical barrier to the transfer of wind and bird-borne afflictions and drift from spraying in adjacent paddocks, however their effectiveness may be limited. There are many ways available to mitigate the impact of insects, isolation of the grove is one as demonstrated by the groves set up in the desert in Peru. Control of access to the grove is another, quarantining the grove and imposing strict protocols on any vehicles such as harvesters entering, as well as any personnel. A 'closed' grove is far more likely to maintain a relatively disease-free status through reduced traffic.

Tree Density and Grove Layout

Following the decision to start out as an organic or non-organic grove comes the critical issue of tree density and grove layout. Simple practical considerations are often missed such as providing adequate turning space at the end of each row for large vehicles like over-the-row harvesters.

Tree density can vary from the traditional 12 metre x 12 metre spacing adopted in very dry climates where nutrient and water availability is low to the super high-density carpet-like plantings. Tree numbers range from around 300 per hectare to some super/ultra high-density groves at 1,600 to 2,200 trees per hectare. A degree of cynicism may be justified when reading the glowing reports on the super high-density groves from the companies which are selling the systems and the trees. Despite the higher establishment costs the groves are promoted as costing less to manage in terms of inputs and harvesting with earlier returns on investment. The groves must be trellised and are still early in their development with too few independent reviews and audits on the horticultural and environmental impact and return on investment. The nurseries producing the specially bred varieties sell many more trees and do not make their money out of selling olive oil. Research this option very carefully and don't be seduced by the glowing promotional events and information presented by those who have a vested interest in everything in the process other than producing and selling olive oil. There are still important issues to overcome such as the mechanical pruning and the long-term productivity of the trees planted in hedge-like rows.

In Spain and Portugal there are serious concerns about the water usage required for these groves. Governments will allocate limited supplies of water to the crops with the highest return per megalitre and olives producing oil will find it hard to compete with other fruit crops and some annual crops. High dependency on large amounts of water will also cause problems in drought where water availability is limited and, if available, very expensive.

In Australia a very large producer received concessional water rights for their grove when it was established. These rights were sold off when the company acquiring them during a liquidation settlement needed cash flow to finance the purchase of the groves. Subsequently, the groves were irrigated with water purchased from the investors who had acquired substantial water rights and traded them annually like a commodity. Irrigators generally have a basic allotment which is adjusted each year based on the water flows and availability in the main rivers. The owners of the water rights are not necessarily farmers and generate substantial income from their investment. During recent drought years and poor water flows in the main rivers the price of water increased to levels where groves were spending tens of millions of dollars to purchase their water requirements. The company which sold off its water rights was severely affected and became one of the leading voices in the campaign for government to rescind laws allowing private ownership of water rights and return to a pool from which water is allocated to irrigators at controlled prices or through an auction system. Another case of karma, the company involved owned the nursery which sold the unproven barnea variety to many producers, including the corporation which it acquired with the water rights subsequently sold off.

There are other unexpected environmental impacts which may have an effect on the claims of easier management. In Spain and Portugal where the groves are harvested at night with very bright arc lights, migratory birds get disoriented and are harvested along with the olives, reputedly being killed in their millions. Many species of birds seasonally migrate between the United Kingdom and North Africa with an overnight rest and recuperation stopover in the olive groves of the Iberian Peninsula. Consumer concern, especially in the United Kingdom, has forced some olive oil brands to refuse to buy olive oil from groves which harvest at night and in 2020 the Portuguese government banned night harvesting. Spain has followed suit in some regions. The resulting 12-hour reduction in harvesting times will push up the cost and lead to less-than-ideal timing with regard to oil accumulation.

Concentration of any living species can lead to easier transmission of disease whatever the vector. The world has recently experienced this with the Covid-19 pandemic with social distancing and dispersal of populations being the primary tactic to avoid rapid spread. With trees the same applies with close proximity facilitating replication and spread of fungal, viral and bacterial disease, and insect pests. Buffer zones established to halt the spread of the bacterium Xylella fastidiosa in olives are the botanical equivalent of human social distancing. The disease which continues to devastate groves in Puglia in Italy at great monetary and social cost has caused mass removal of trees in attempts to limit its spread.

The high concentration of trees planted in the high-density and super high- density groves make them incubators for disease and breeding grounds for pests, especially when they are in close proximity to other plantations. Add to this the relatively low disease resistance gauged by the polyphenol levels in the fruit of the favoured dwarf varieties for high-density planting - arbequina, arbosana, and koreneiki - and you have a potential disease problem. This can be mitigated with regular spraying with fungicides, bactericides and pesticides which is expensive and increases the risk of exceeding maximum residue levels in the final product if the correct withdrawal periods are not adhered to.

The planting of varieties low in polyphenol levels will result in the olive oils produced from these groves being lower in health benefits and having shorter shelf-life than other more robust oils. This may result in lower prices usually offered for these 'blending' oils often used to bulk-up the oils with high polyphenol counts such as picual.

The high-density systems were initiated in Spain in the 1990's and in the lifespan of the olive tree this is a short history which does not give a fair indication of the longevity and continued productivity of these plantings. They may lose productivity in 20-30 years and must be replanted, good for the nurseries supplying trees but costly for the producer. The publicity given to super high-density plantings may lead a prospective producer to believe that it is already the preferred method. This is not the case with a relatively small area of the groves in Spain being planted to super high-density and estimates in Jaen province suggest only 40-50% can be converted to modern high-density groves given the terrain and other environmental considerations such as water supply. The small size of the holdings means the change will need major socio-economic adjustments with aggregation of holdings and shared management and equipment. The independence of farmers may make this hurdle more difficult to clear than the horticultural challenges.

Our grove was planted in the early days of the development of high-density groves, super high-density configurations were still a few years in the future. We opted for a compromise with planting spacing of 9 metres by 4.5 metres. Water is a limiting factor on our farm and made planting a high-density grove with spacing of 4.5m x 4.5m too risky. The 9m x 4.5m spacing gave us the option of planting an extra row between the existing rows, doubling the tree population if we found that the water available would allow this. In fact, we did interplant every fifth row with rows containing a mixture of varieties we wanted to trial for future plantings and to act as pollinators.

Having estimated that 10,000 trees was the minimum requirement for a financially viable enterprise, we decided to plant in two stages to manage the risk of making errors in the first planting of 5,000 trees. Another risk management decision which later proved sensible was to plant a mixture of varieties for oil production and table olive production.

Early in the research for the budget it became apparent that the price we could expect to receive for oil at AU$4 per kilogram (kg) was the same as that we should receive for table olives at AU$4 per kg. The density of olive oil varies around 0.910, a fact which is important when trading and calculating prices. Trade quotations for oil are usually in kilograms while smaller enterprises often quote in $ per litre. This transposition has caused many disputes in purchasing contracts.

We worked out that at a 20% oil yield and AU$4/kg we would receive AU$80 for the oil from 100kg of olives. Assuming a 20% loss of mass during the processing of table olives (compared with 80% loss in oil processing) for 100kg of table olives at AU$4/kg we would receive AU$320, four times as much as our potential receipts for oil. The processing of the table olives would require less capital investment if we decided to install processing facilities.

All these decisions can be justified as we look back at 25 years of production. Water has always been an issue and we could not have sustained a high-density planting. For the first planting of 2,000 trees we ordered 600 mission, 600 manzanilla, 500 kalamata, and 300 verdale. We ordered from three different nurseries. Four years after planting with the first fruit we discovered that the 600 mission were in fact verdale so we ended up with 900 verdale, an olive with low oil yield and only good for green table olives, despite having a large pit. The second planting of 3,000 trees allowed us to plant corregiolo as a high yielding, well acclimatised, oil variety, nevadillo blanco and more kalamata along with many pollinators. We had no recourse for the supply of the wrong variety which happened again to a small degree with the second planting where some arbequina were mixed up with the corregiolo. We have also switched to table olive production while oil prices are low knowing we can always switch back to olive oil production.

The lessons are to build flexibility into the configuration of your planting and manage the risk of some inputs like water being limited through cost or availability. When selecting varieties consider dual purpose olives for both green and black table olives which also yield high oil percentages. Finally, don't trust olive tree nurseries to deliver the varieties you ordered. Check the mother trees from which they take cuttings, scrutinise their quality control and contingencies to avoid mixing the cuttings and have a clause in your purchase agreement that they will replace any trees which do not meet your order and cover the cost of replacing trees already planted along with loss of production.

Our decision to plant our trees in stages as we learned the vagaries of the industry was sensible. We stopped at 5,500 trees, finding that we could manage the smaller number with minimal inputs and maintain a profit margin without taking substantial risk of crop failure or falling prices. As you will read, we found other ways of developing the enterprise which supplemented the income from the grove.

Recently we have been a little indulgent by collecting all the self-propagated trees in the grove and planting them out in rows, adding around 600 to our tree population. These trees are cross-pollinated from our varieties and will provide an interesting array of vegetation and fruit. In the early days of our venture, we travelled the immediate locality collecting and propagating cuttings from various olive trees growing wild and those which are growing around the gardens and churches. The latter were brought here from coastal towns where migrants from Europe had established them. The 'church' olives produce a lovely round fruit which makes an excellent table olive which we have dubbed the 'Blessed Olives'. We have no idea what the varieties of the purloined cuttings were, their progeny are now dotted around the grove and their development keenly observed. Who knows, from our cross-pollinated trees we may find a new varietal worth propagating en masse.

Harvesting and Pruning

The harvesting method and pruning practices are more considerations in grove planning. Hand harvesting, hand-held rakes, shakers or tractor driven or self-propelled harvesters are all available. Your choice will depend on whether you are producing olive oil or table olives, availability, cost of labour and equipment, and timing.

Children, family and friends are helpful when it comes to hand harvesting. In Mediterranean countries harvesting is traditionally a time of celebration when families gather to do the toil and enjoy the sheer bliss of the newly pressed extra virgin olive oil. When harvest is over, they return home with containers of fresh olive oil for use until the next harvest.

Traditional harvesting of olives for oil is usually done with long sticks or 'batone' with which the trees are beaten to dislodge the fruit which falls onto nets laid out on the ground under the tree. In Greece this practice is supplemented with cutting branches off and running them through a comb-like machine to remove fruit. The branches are those which will eventually be pruned, olives left on the tree are beaten with sticks or removed with a hand-held mechanical comb. The next step up is a hand-held shaker which is attached to a branch and vibrates to dislodge the fruit. Having used one of these the impression is that the user gets well shaken too. In our grove for table olive production, we keep the trees low to the ground and use hand-held rakes stripping the olives onto nets or using gloved hands to pluck them into specially shaped harvesting buckets. Green olives are easily bruised so are treated more gently than the black olives which do not show the bruising.

In newly established groves not held by tradition where family and friends provide the labour, the novelty of harvest wears off after a few years. Then one can resort to making it an event with copious amounts of food and wine at the end of the day when the harvesting is done. Soon the party becomes more of an attraction than harvesting with the 'free' labour diminishing and the tolerance of the producer being tested. Finally, it becomes necessary to adjust the management to harvest oneself over a longer period, purchase a harvesting machine or engage a contract harvester.

Hand harvesting can be used with almost any planting configuration and pruning shape. It is the most expensive harvesting method; the upside is that the fruit is relatively undamaged when it goes to the mill for oil extraction or into the fermentation barrels for pickling. Mobile machine harvesting demands more attention to the shape of the tree. Tree shakers, either attached to tractors or self-propelled, attach themselves to the trunk and vibrate the tree. The olives can be caught in nets spread out under the tree or in an inverted umbrella-like catcher which folds out under the tree before the shaker is attached to the trunk. Various conveyor mechanisms then transfer the olives to mobile bins for transport to the processor. Owning one of these machines is convenient, especially if it can be attached to the tractor. It allows the producer to harvest at the preferred time, considering factors such as oil accumulation, water and polyphenol levels in the fruit. Owning a complete unit is also expensive as it sits in the shed for most of the year. Bringing in contractors can be costly, the timing is dependent on their other commitments, and they do not necessarily arrive when expected. Delays may be caused by bogging when wet, tight schedules with over-booking or machinery breakdown. This means that the timing of harvest will be less than ideal, and your product may not meet expectation.

Shakers can be used with most tree configurations if there is room to manoeuvre around the tree. The time of day and condition of the tree may also have an impact on the use of some shakers which are attached to the trunk and can dislodge the bark.

For high-density groves and all super high-density groves, over the row harvesters are required. They come small as grape-harvesters which can be used for hedge-like plantings or massive machines which can straddle and harvest taller trees. The same problems can arise with contract harvesters regarding timing, cost and availability. These machines are simply too expensive for smaller groves to own.

Two further factors to consider relating to harvesting efficiency are tree shape and ripeness of the fruit. The two most common systems of pruning are vase and monoconal. Traditional groves are generally pruned in a vase shape which allows the sunlight into the middle of the tree and increases airflow which tends to reduce fungal diseases. This style of pruning is not suitable for over the row harvesting.

Modern high-density groves are pruned in a monoconal style with a central trunk. These groves are suitable for over the row harvesters which use paddles to agitate the tree and dislodge fruit. If the tree spacing allows, shakers can also be used with monoconal pruning.

The second factor is the fruit removal force (FRF) which varies with varieties and the stage of ripeness of the fruit. It is the force required to remove fruit and can be measured with a special instrument. Unripe green olives have a high FRF and very ripe olives are easily removed having a low FRF. Mechanical harvesting tends to become less efficient the higher the FRF and must be taken into consideration when estimating yield as a percentage of the fruit will be left on the tree. With black ripe fruit most of the fruit will be removed. However, the later the harvesting the more prone the fruit is to disease, frost and dislodgement by wind.

There are chemicals which can be sprayed onto the trees which will accelerate ripening and decrease the FRF within 6-10 days of application, resulting in more effective harvesting, both by hand and machine. However, trees can suffer leaf drop and severe weather events can cause fruit drop. Care in using the correct concentrations of the chemicals will avoid denuding the trees of all leaves and fruit!

The experience of the operator should be assessed to maximise harvesting efficiency with machinery and minimise damage to the tree with shakers and uprooting of trees with over the row harvesters.

In some groves the olives are allowed to ripen until they fall on the ground onto nets or are vacuumed up by suction machines. In the latter cases it is inevitable that sand and stones are sucked up as well and must be removed mechanically at the mill prior to entering the extraction line. A high percentage of olive oil is extracted from these very ripe olives; however, it is low quality and will almost certainly be deemed to be lampante requiring refining. Some farmers believe that it is better to receive lower prices for a greater volume of lower grade oil than to invest in costly harvesting and chase the higher prices of extra virgin olive oil, as well as trying to reach the more stringent specifications for this classification. This is their prerogative as there is demand for refined olive oil, mainly used in manufacturing.

Now wc have selected the varieties, the grove planting density and configuration, pruning style, harvesting method and other infrastructure we are ready to plant the grove. Or, if buying an existing grove, we have enough information to assess the potential and return on investment.

There are many technical resources available from agricultural research institutions, associations, online, consultants and nurseries on how to plant a grove, lay out irrigation infrastructure, provide nutrients and control weeds, pests and diseases. It is not the intention to provide technical information other than advise the sourcing of information from multiple sources – local producers, institutions, advisers and any other independent reputable provider.

While the grove is growing there are many activities which can be undertaken to improve the chances of producing a product which will sell well and return a profit.

There is no doubt knowledge is a powerful aid to making the right decisions and developing the correct approach to the myriad of situations which will confront a producer of extra virgin, or other classifications of, olive oil and table olives. Time spent in increasing our industry awareness and professional development is never wasted and the knowledge acquired will give a competitive edge in the marketplace.

Awareness

Passion is a word often used in the olive oil industry when describing a commitment to use and promotion of extra virgin olive oil. It is a powerful and compelling emotion which often blinds the person to the realities of the product and trade in olive oil. Passion combined with the knowledge on how and where to direct this energy will lead to a productive and profitable enterprise. Profit here is used in its broadest sense of a gain, not necessarily financial.

Knowledge of your product, and that of competing products, is an essential foundation to positioning and selling the olive oil which your newly acquired or established grove will be producing.

Learning About the Product and Market

Two tools are useful in rationalising where to spend time in learning about the product and market.

The first is the marketing funnel which graphically represents the process of promoting your product to a buyer, eventually leading to a sale. The funnel has five stages: awareness, consideration, conversion, loyalty and advocacy. The aperture or top of the funnel depicts the broad campaign to attract potential customers with the rationalisation of these leads to a more concentrated conversion and loyalty phase. This process applies to the industry with international marketing undertaken by global entities, the International Olive Council based in Madrid in the case of olive oil. Under this umbrella there will be national, regional, local and brand marketing and sales. We will look at these various tiers in some detail.

The second is an understanding of the essential elements of a competitive industry: suppliers, buyers, competitors, new entrants and substitutes. In this you are a new entrant and therefore probably seen as a threat to established enterprises. This is an attitude prevalent in the olive oil industry where other producers or traders are seen as a threat and competition. The fifth element, substitutes, suggests how destructive this combative approach can be. While producers, regions and countries fight amongst themselves in the olive oil trading world, substitutes are available, and more are being engineered or developed all the time. An example is avocado oil. To minimise the threat of substitutes eroding the olive oil market, the industry must show unity of purpose to hold and expand its share in the vegetable oil market.

Accusations of fraud and other deceitful activities between olive producing regions receive a lot of publicity. In this era of social media one incident involving a small quantity of fraudulent oil can receive multiple and repetitive publicity worldwide over months giving the impression that fraud is rife.

Even at local level it is common for a producer to talk down a neighbour's brand using no more than a personal opinion on its quality, often fuelled by antagonism. The damage done to the industry by this internecine trade warfare is extensive and continuing. It opens the market to the competing vegetable oils. It is incumbent on suppliers, buyers and competitors within the olive oil industry to realise that they must put the interests and future of the entire industry first if it is to be successful and expand to give larger market share to olive oil, better prices and greater profitability. The industry should also welcome new entrants who bring new energy, ideas, innovation and investment. If the olive industry does not actively attract these new entrants with their intellectual and financial capital, they may well go to competing vegetable oil industries.

As an individual participant in the olive oil industry anywhere along the supply chain, or as a service provider, the greatest service you can do for yourself and your industry is to develop an intimate knowledge of your product, olive oil. This knowledge will not only give you an advantage in selling your products, but also help you contribute to an objective discussion on future directions of the industry worldwide and defend your products from false information designed to undermine its integrity.

Before purchasing or establishing your grove, you probably had good reasons for taking the plunge: investment, lifestyle, passion, sea change and many others. This was probably followed with research through associations, online and other sources. You may have been seduced by the positive promotions of nurseries, service suppliers and associations. This is fair as all industries need new entrants for growth. It is up to you to test the validity of the claims and the merits of various production systems.

There is one claim which you will no doubt hear many times. Insert the brand, locality, region, country, competition as appropriate in '.......... produces the best extra virgin olive oil in the world' or '............. competition awards the best extra virgin olive oils in the world'. So, there are many 'best' olive oils in the world. There is no best, there are thousands of excellent extra virgin olive oils produced in most regions and the difference between the top tier of oils as judged in competitions is always small and often subjective. Ask any producer or distributor which is the world's best olive oil and they will say 'ours' – with associated passion!

As the revived olive oil production reached the supermarkets and boutique stores, industry protagonists in Australia repeatedly made claims that Australian olive oil was the best in the world. Similar headlines greeted consumers when the results of competitions were announced. In the newly revived industry, the oils were judged by judges who were relatively inexperienced by world standards. The judges of most competitions were mainly producers, there is no competition, to our knowledge worldwide, which is judged entirely by consumers who purchase the olive oil for domestic use.

It seemed ridiculous that a country where production was mainly from young immature groves managed by relatively inexperienced personnel was able to catapult its product in a few years to be amongst the best in the world. This jingoistic approach lulled producers into the false sense of security of not needing to continuously improve their product because it is so good already. Most of the new producing countries or regions demonstrated this complacency and some still do; Australia, New Zealand, South Africa, California, China and others.

Unable to reconcile this claim with the Mediterranean countries having cumulative knowledge acquired over centuries with the world's best technical research, we decided to set out to find the world’s best extra virgin olive oils and learn about them. As related earlier we engaged with Judy Ridgway to develop Extra Virgin Olive Oil Savantes. We engaged Judy as a consultant and presenter of the Savantes programmes, initially in Australia then overseas. In the early years her influence and presence helped establish the integrity of the programme and set the positive style of tasting. The philosophy of the training has remained unchanged twenty years later. After a while Judy’s involvement became less frequent as the number of Savantes events increased. The longevity of the Savantes programme is testament to the practical and independent ethos which Judy helped establish.

With the generous cooperation of producers of brands selected for their diversity, quality and consistency as judged by the world’s leading competitions, in Savantes we taste a broad spectrum of styles and flavours of extra virgin olive oils from many varieties and regions. The programmes start with a presentation of the global olive oil market trends. This is followed by sessions on the classification and regulations pertaining to international trade. The tasting sessions explore the range of styles and flavours of extra virgin olive oil. The participants are encouraged to understand and learn the expanse of their own tasting ability and vocabulary to describe flavours in terms of food. A session explores the traditional and modern uses of olive oil in food and other processes. The health attributes are discussed at length and the relation of the benefits to quality. Blending sessions take a whole day and invariably build the confidence of the attendees as they work in groups. The value and integrity of many competitions is discussed with analysis presented to demonstrate the bias and inconsistency of some of the judging. Various exercises which can be undertaken during personal training are presented and, after a virtual tour of the world tasting olive oils from regions, the olive oils brought by participants are tasted and evaluated.

There are some rules covering the programme and presentation of oils which are sacrosanct to the Savantes ethos. The olive oils are tasted blind with the details and brands only revealed after the tasting and discussion. If an oil is considered defective its brand is not revealed and a communication is later sent to the producer suggesting that the oil is tested by an official panel. It is not the place of Savantes to classify oils as defective or otherwise. The olive oil brands are not promoted, and the preference of the presenters is not revealed. The question is always asked 'What is your favourite oil', or 'Do you like the oil'. The answers are invariably that there are no favourites, and we are not interested in personal preferences, just objective assessment and description. Savantes receives no financial support other than the registration fees and does not receive sponsorship from any source. The producers of the olive oils supply the oils at their own expense. In return the oils are treated with respect and an objective evaluation and tasting notes are sent after the sessions. The tasting notes can be published unedited by the producers. The contact details of all the producers are provided to the participants and a list of extra virgin olive oils placed on the Savantes website.

Our objective with Savantes is to first encourage olive oil tasting in the market context and be realistic about the commercial prospects. Then give an idea of the range of products available in terms of flavour and packaging. The olive oils are used as a vehicle to enhance attendees tasting ability, recognising that there is no right or wrong in tasting, we all have different reference points, palates and experience, all of which are valid.

Defects in the Product

With respect to the detection of defects, unlike some institutions which are involved in technical training, we deal with positive characteristics of olive oil first. The International Olive Oil Council (IOC) administers nearly 80 tasting panels around the world accredited to classify olive oil. These IOC technical panels form the backbone of tasting and many of the tasters are judges in competitions. At least eight tasters in these panels must be involved in the classification of an oil. The IOC conducts ring tests each year to test the competency of panels in detecting and describing the intensity of defects and the positive attributes of fruitiness, bitterness and pepperiness (pungency) of an extra virgin olive oil. The ring test comprises sending out several identical samples to all the panels and collating their tasting evaluation to test conformity. An annual series of ring tests is used to validate the panels' competency with accreditation being granted or removed predicated on the results being within a stipulated range. Scrutiny of the results of these ring tests reveals that even within highly trained panels there is considerable variation in the identity and intensity evaluation of defective oils. In effect the defect classifications are determined through averaging the sensory analysis of 80 panels of eight tasters, with panels exhibiting outlier evaluations losing their accreditation.

We in Savantes do not consider it our only remit to train and encourage tasters to detect and describe the degree of defect. We are fortunate and grateful that the IOC provides us with fresh samples of defects for our events. This in no way indicates any endorsement by the IOC of the Savantes programme, however, sensibly it means that our participants learn using the genuine defect.

The panel system for classification for olive oil is a subject of continuing debate. There is tension between the technicians who advocate its objectivity and the trade which sees it as subjective, often inconsistent, and limiting their profitability. The process is too slow for quick decisions on sales and purchases predicated on quality. Research to find laboratory-based analytical procedures to detect defects are ongoing and partially successful, however, the current consensus is that the panel test may be imperfect, but it is the best the industry has to assess quality at the moment.

Savantes promulgates the view that the industry attitude worldwide which specifies the detection of defects first in olive oil evaluation and classification sends the wrong message. It is like driving along a road concentrating on avoiding potholes, thereby missing the magnificent views unfolding along the way. If the first view of anything you are asked to comment on is to try to find faults, you will generally find them. This encourages a culture whereby individual tasters, who may be inexperienced, will declare an olive oil defective when it is not, it is a new flavour which the taster has not come across before. In other words, the default classification is 'fault'.

With the ubiquitous social media platforms available there are many posts where tasters, often after a relatively short course of taste training, promote themselves to be experts. The courses by way of promoting themselves advertise that at the end of a course or series of short courses the taster is a 'master taster' or 'expert'. With most courses there is no competency test which must be passed for certification as a competent taster, and no continuing assessment to ensure the 'certified' taster maintains their knowledge and skill.

There is a lot of damage done to brands and the industry at large by individuals deemed experts taking olive oils off the shelves, tasting them on their own or with friends and then publishing the results and naming the brands which they consider defective or non-conforming.

Recognising Competent Tasters

The IOC does not certify or accredit individual tasters as it would seem to conflict with their dictum that only a trained and annually tested panel of eight tasters can classify oils. The void created by the absence of an official register of tasters with associated competency tests has allowed the burgeoning range of tasting courses available in many producing and consuming countries. Our approaches to the IOC to introduce a national certification system were not successful. So, as we do, we decided to introduce a system founded on sound competency standards. We not only wanted to recognise excellence as tasters, but also to encourage the knowledge of varietals from different regions.

Through Savantes we started to train a panel according to the IOC method in Australia and subsequently decided that while the training was beneficial, we were not comfortable with the remit to technically classify defects and intensities. We considered a more commercial approach to recognition of expertise and, having been the project manager for the writing of competency standards for agricultural scientists in Australia, we set about writing competency standards for olive oil experts.

We introduced recognition as a Member of the Register of International Extra Virgin Olive Oil Savantes for those who could provide evidence that they met the highest competency requirements. The evidence-based process was ponderous and time-consuming with only three tasters achieving Savante status. Three years later in 2012 we introduced the Savante Skills Test which tests tasting ability, fault detection and knowledge of varietals. In 90 minutes, the candidate must work through 38 oils comprising intensity rankings, fault detection, triangle tests and variety identification. Two levels of recognition were introduced, Extra Virgin Olive Oil Savante and Associate Savante. The score for the technical exercises of rankings, triangle tests and fault detection enable the achievement of Associate Savante. To become a Savante, a reasonable score in the variety identification is also required. The philosophy behind the two levels is to distinguish between good technical tasters and authoritative tasters. The tests were taken at the end of our three-day training programmes and initially the results were poor. We thought that the tests may be too difficult and considered making them easier. However, we persisted with the breakthrough coming when we attached the tests to other events and started getting more experienced tasters participating.

At the first Spanish Team Tasting Championship held in conjunction with the Association for Quality Control of the Oils of the Region of Priego de Córdoba in Spain, we presented the first Savante Certificate and many Associate Savante Certificates. The celebration following the first achievement of Savante justified the degree of difficulty and the uncompromising attention to consistency in the setting of the tests, wherever the location. The kudos attached by the tasters was gratifying in confirming that the Savante recognition of individual competence had standing in Spain, the world's largest producer of olive oil. On one occasion in Priego de Cordoba after the most recently recognised Savante had dispensed the traditional duty of buying a round of drinks, he departed to congratulatory applause as the competitors lined the side of the bar to the exit.

The following year a taster in New York, Joanne Lacina of Olive Oil Lovers, achieved a perfect score in the test, an extraordinary display of tasting competence and knowledge of the world's main varieties. There are now full members of the Savantes Register in Spain, USA, South Africa, France and Greece. Associate Savantes reside in all those countries as well as Netherlands, Ireland, Portugal, Canada, New Zealand and Australia.

Savantes and Associates are involved in the entire olive industry from production through to distribution, research, trading, retail, administration and education. From small beginnings the network is now truly international and fostering knowledge and respect across borders and regions.

To recognise those who repeatedly demonstrate their competency we have introduced the Silver, Gold and Platinum Frequent Tasters Associate Savante Certification. There are two Platinum Associates who have achieved Associate status four times. This consistency in tasting deserves greater recognition and we have resolved to elevate Platinum Associates to full Savante status when they achieve the Associate score for the fifth time.

Overcoming Regional Rivalry

There is much rivalry and bias between regions which needs to be overcome if we are to present a cohesive and united message to consumers. Too often we hear of Italians denigrating Spanish oil and vice versa. The same occurs with Greek oils and more recently as they have become major producers, Tunisian oils are the butt of derision. This is unproductive as all extra virgin olive oils have their place in a market where a range of qualities and flavours is needed. Nurturing new entrant countries will help increase the supply and provide a broader ethnic and financial base to promote extra virgin olive oil.

Through the many training programmes we have presented in 11 countries with thousands of participants we have found that recognition of flavours from varietals from different regions needs improvement. Lack of knowledge often leads to denunciation as defective, usually rancidity. We find this particularly when Spanish tasters who are used to robust bitter and peppery olive oils taste the more delicate and nutty varieties such as koroneiki from Greece, l'aglandau from France and chemlali from Tunisia.

To overcome this, we set out to hold team tasting championships where teams of three tasters compete by undertaking the Savantes Skills Test as individuals, followed by team tests which include pairing oils from varietals grown in different regions, for example; coratina from Italy and Australia, koroneiki from Greece and Spain and picholine from France and New Zealand. The events are edifying, competitive and convivial. After three national championships in Spain and one in each of Greece, France and the USA, a World Team Tasting Championship was held in Priego de Cordoba where the initial support for the concept emanated from the Denomination of Origin Association (PDO) and local producers. The World Championship attracted 13 teams from Spain, France, Greece, South Africa and Netherlands. A team from Navarra in Spain became the first world champions.

The event presented some difficulties especially with the technical assessment of the quality of the olive oils to be used. The classification as extra virgin of several oils from Greece, Tunisia and France was questioned by a small panel of Spanish tasters and could not be used. Being held in September the oils were almost a year old. This reduced the available oils leaving no option but to use oils in which some of the competitors had an interest. This is a situation which we will try and avoid in the future by having more producing countries represented on the panel which screens the oils. We do not need the debate caused by this issue detracting from the excellent performance of the winning teams. However, with many tasters being producers, consultants or working for large corporations, it may be difficult to avoid inclusion of oils to which they may have a connection.

Another question which we will address is whether oils or competitors should be excluded from this high-profile event because they are in some way associated with a high quality and differentiated oil. Unlike a competition awarding the oils, in this instance a third party is setting the tests and the competitors have no direct input. Knowing that their oil has been submitted for inclusion and not knowing where and if it has been used can be just as confusing. In a later chapter we will have more to say about judges knowingly entering their products in competitions in which they are judging.

The impact of the Championships has achieved a wider knowledge of the varietals around the world. It has shown regions which thought that they had exclusivity in producing a particular varietal and style of oil that this is no longer the case. At the inaugural French championship, a competitor accused the organisers of spreading misinformation by including an oil from the coratina variety which had been produced in Australia. The words were to the effect that 'everyone knows that coratina extra virgin olive oils are only produced in the Puglia region of Italy'. Added to this alleged transgression was the revelation that another coratina used in the varietal pairing team test was processed in Tuscany, the freshly harvested olives having been trucked in a refrigerated container from Puglia overnight and processed the next day. The label of this coratina oil, which won the best oil on show award in international competition in the USA three years in a row, clearly stated the provenance of the product as is required by law. The outstanding extra virgin olive oil was processed by one of the world's most expert and respected millers. This is an example of the bias and parochialism which the Savantes programmes strive to overcome.

There are generally two common reactions to the championships; some teams and the panels they represent see the exposure to different products as a challenge with the acquired knowledge giving them a better understanding of the market and more efficient assessment of olive oils submitted for classification. Others found the disappointment of not achieving a Savante status or faring well as a team was embarrassing and instead of acknowledging that they need to improve, trying to change the championship to tilt it in their favour. One coorganiser in a particular country refused to hold another championship unless the tests were modified to make them easier and only regional varieties used. Some competitors were unhappy about the varieties from different countries, with which they were not familiar, being used. We note that some of these team members are judges in the international competitions which include varieties from around the world. We hope that they use that opportunity to improve their recognition of the flavours from different regions and varieties and become better judges. The expectation was that Savantes certification would still be provided for the modified championships. Acceding to this would undermine the purpose of the national championships.

It is surprising that some tasting panels from different regions are not more active in evaluating varieties from new entrants such as Tunisia with the chemlali and chetoui varietals. Coming onto the market in large volumes, extra virgin olive oil from Tunisia is replacing olive oils from Greece in blends. The olive oils have a reasonably similar flavour profile to koroneiki oils and are cheaper. Continuing the theme of product knowledge, it would seem wise for panels which advise local producers on blending and style to be expansive in obtaining samples of competing varieties to monitor competition.

An unexpected benefit of the World Team Championships is the conviviality of the event with the friendships and mutual respect generated. The hosts in Priego de Cordoba made the championships edifying and fun the way only the Spanish do. We are grateful for their support and hope to return there for a championship in the post-covid world. We subscribe to the comments that tasting is taken too seriously and panel membership has become too much of a status symbol. Tasting should be fun, more on that later.

Olive Oil as an Ingredient

Extra virgin olive oil is a food ingredient and, apart from the daily tablespoon of raw olive oil taken by some who believe it is beneficial for their health, it is used in cooking. Anyone who has staffed a stand at a trade show will know that the public are not used to tasting raw olive oil, or any raw vegetable oil for that matter. Tasting olive oil is an acquired taste and mostly used by trainers and traders to explore the flavours and other characteristics such as viscosity or mouthfeel. Some consumers are happy to use bread to dip into the oil and savour the flavour. A marketer of a well-known Spanish brand of extra virgin olive oil attended our course in New York prior to the Summer Fancy Food Show. During the culinary presentation in the course it is suggested that at trade shows potential customers are given the option of tasting the product in food or tasting it raw. The premise is that if we can get consumers to associate flavours with food it is more suggestive than the technical flavour description of the taste profile. The course participant went on to try the food association at Summer Fancy Food and sent a text message to the effect that there was substantially increased interest at the stand.

Tasting olive oil raw in a tasting glass is very different from tasting it in food where it interacts with the other food ingredients. As an exercise we presented participants at an olive industry conference in Chicago with some cookies made with canola oil, refined olive oil, olive pomace oil, a delicate extra virgin olive oil, a robust extra virgin olive oil and a rancid olive oil. We asked them to name the cookies made with the different oils, given that the rest of the ingredients were identical. They found it very difficult, as it is. In addition to the taste differences there were differences in colour and texture.

This exercise prompted the exploration of a new series of courses and competency tests under the banner of Culinary Savantes. We developed some simple cooking and food matching exercises with participants working as individuals and in groups. The course would culminate with a test requiring; naming the varieties of extra virgin olive oils in dishes, the intensity rankings in food, detecting the difference where refined, pomace, virgin and extra virgin olive oil was used in the same dish and detection of defective olive oils in food. Those achieving the prescribed score would be awarded certification as Associate Culinary Savante or Culinary Savante. In the group exercises there would be a competitive element with each group preparing a dish from different cuisines – Chinese, Japanese, Asian, Indian, Mexican and others. The groups would then taste and score the dishes. The intention here is to expand the culinary vocabulary beyond the Mediterranean diet to explore the use of olive oil in emerging markets.

We committed two years of meetings to organise this with various commercial and/or educational culinary enterprises in the USA, United Kingdom, France, Spain, Italy, Greece and Australia. The meetings revealed a lot about the attitude, understanding and commitment to using extra virgin olive oil. Collectively the cost, risk, mono-cuisine culture, lack of facilities and a level of indifference has resulted in this concept being shelved until a partner can be found to support the culinary concepts and mitigate the costs to participants. Our commitment to the concept has not diminished as the association of extra virgin olive oil with food across all cuisines is of paramount importance in increasing the use of extra virgin olive oil worldwide

Food Pairing and Oleacuisiniers

When talking about the flavour of varieties during tasting programmes there are two questions which are frequently asked. The first is how to match olive oils to dishes and cuisine? Much is made of this food pairing, and some like to call themselves 'olive oil sommeliers' and offer courses as such. The word sommelier comes from the wine industry and has been hijacked by the olive oil purveyors to create a mystique about the knowledge of extra virgin olive oil and how it should be used. There are many instances where the olive industry is compared to the wine industry in the hope that extra virgin olive oil will take on the omnipresence of wine in food culture. A couple of bottles of olive oil will not be consumed with a meal or at home as the universal relaxant. Pursuing this comparison seems a little pretentious and can lead to some false expectations from consumers. The set of wine aromas sold for training is sometimes used for familiarising tasters with the method of detecting and describing aroma in extra virgin olive oil. This does not make sense if the connection of olive oil flavour and aroma with food is to be developed and highlighted.

It would be smart to adopt another word specific to olive oil which describes the practice of matching with food ingredients. If the word included 'olive' or a derivative it would give the practice more substance. Something like 'oleacuisinier' or 'cuisinierolea'?

The second common question is whether there is a universal reference or guide which provides the taster with the dominant flavours of extra virgin olive oil from different varieties? There is a diagrammatic flavour wheel which can be used as a prompt while trying to detect flavours when tasting. There are also some books which attempt to list the flavours to be found in extra virgin olive oils from varieties. The problem with these is that they tend to standardise the flavours tasters find and become a shortcut. There is no substitute for the enjoyable hard work of tasting as many olive oils as possible and learning the general flavours which can be expected in a variety. General because our palates and vocabulary are all different and flavours change from region and season and there is no rigid rule. There are some tips which will help identify the nuances of different varieties and they are personal to your palate.

As a new entrant to the industry there is the opportunity to develop ancillary activities to increase your knowledge, presence and competitiveness in preparation for the launch of your product into the market. The development of Savantes demonstrates that a training product can be successful competing in the countries where similar programmes have been offered for many years. The key elements for success are differentiation and integrity. The Savantes programme differentiates itself by treating quality product with respect, showing no favour to any region, providing a certification which sets a high standard and is sought after, and treating olive oil as a commercial product by always working within the marketing framework.

In the time for contemplation provided by the enforced lockdowns of the pandemic we have experimented with innovative tasting methods for the graphical presentation of flavours. The result of this period of experimentation is the Savantes Savourgram© which was launched in 2022. Before introducing this innovation in olive oil flavour profiling, I will describe the pre-pandemic Savantes rubric.

To demonstrate the use of all our senses while tasting, prior to Savantes programmes an alphabet of aroma is purchased from the local grocery or food store. The foods cover twenty-six, or A-Z, of the fruit, vegetable, herb, nut and spice aromas found in the extra virgin olive oils to be tasted. Prior to shopping, all the oils, which can number up to 60 for a three-day course, are tasted and notes taken of the aromas and tastes. Purchasing the food locally ensures the ingredients are available in the region. There is a tendency to describe the flavours of olive oil with reference to ingredients in Mediterranean or Western food. This practice needs to change if we are to encourage the use of olive oil in Asian, Indian, Mexican and other cuisines. Paying attention to the ethnicity of the participants undertaking taste training and adapting the taste descriptions accordingly will lead to use with their cooking.

The ingredients used for aroma training should be spread equally across the fruit, vegetable, spice, nut and herb spectrum and cut-up or placed into opaque containers and covered with cloth such as muslin or cloth kitchen wipes so the taster cannot see the ingredients. The exercise is for the individual to smell the contents of the containers from A-Z and identify the ingredients. It is rare for a score of over 50% to be achieved and tasters are surprised how much removal of the visual stimulus affects their ability to describe the aroma of an ingredient which they use regularly. This demonstrates the need to develop the aroma vocabulary and train the brain to discern and describe aromas in olive oil where there is no visual stimulus, just oil. This is one of many exercises which can be used outside formal training to sharpen tasting skill.

Another discipline which, if practised, will become second nature is to think flavour whenever eating and try to identify the tastes of the individual ingredients in any food you eat. Generally, people take a forkful of the food, put it in their mouth and just chew it as a homogenous mass without appreciating the taste of the individual ingredients contributing to the overall flavour. Sharpening tasting ability will greatly enhance your enjoyment of good fresh food, unfortunately the downside is that you will also detect more off-flavours or stale ingredients, especially those that are rancid. Your shopping behaviour will change, and you will seek out fresher food and shun brands which sell product which is rancid, stale or tasteless.

The flavour wheel which summarises the aroma and tastes of olive oil neatly in the food groups diagrammatically is a useful tool, but like the list of flavours from varietals we do not encourage dependency on it. We prefer that the taster visualises a supermarket or grocery food display and mentally works through the sections to trigger the aroma or flavour description detected in the oil. If the oil is fruity, work through the fruit section, it may be tropical fruit like banana or melon, or stone fruit like peach or plum. The vegetal aromas and bitter tastes could be herbs, salad vegetables, avocado, cabbage or tomato (which is a fruit!). Go through the spice section with chilli, or pepper, and then there are the crossovers – spicy and bitter vegetables like rocket, arugula, mustard, nasturtium leaves and cress. The nutty taste usually found at the finish of the olive oil could be almond, walnut which is usually a little tannic, macadamia or pecan. Build your vocabulary and be inquisitive about the aromas and taste of ingredients you have not come across before, or do not use frequently.

In Savantes we encourage tasters first to smell the aroma of the olive oil and decide whether it reminds them of fruit, vegetable, herbs, nuts, spices or any other food. This can be the first indicator of the variety and time of harvesting. A taster who has tasted a range of extra virgin olive oils will start to think about varieties which exhibit the dominant aroma.

A useful training exercise to build the aroma vocabulary is to cut up food, for example a lettuce salad, or fruit salad, and place it in the cobalt blue tasting glass which is the specially designed ‘cup’ used for technical olive oil tasting. The aroma emanating from the cup will give you a reference point for distinguishing the different aromas of olive oil and help with the initial determination of the aroma to a food group or groups. In many cases the olive oil will have aromas from two or more food groups and can be described as vegetal and spicy, or fruity and nutty.

Next, we encourage the taster to think of the progression of tastes which they discern as the oil moves from the front to the back of the mouth and then in the throat. We use the chromosome as a metaphor trying to describe the tastes which are represented by the different gene sequences in a chromosome map. This resonates and the taster starts to discern patterns of tastes for each oil. With experience these patterns become a map for different varieties, the main roads stay the same, but the size or intensity may vary and the minor roads will change, some may be signposted others not. The signposts are prior experiences, the roads without signposts are the new ones worth exploring.

A personal example may help understand this concept. For my palate the hojiblanca variety has a particular nuance which is apparent whether the extra virgin olive oil comes from Priego de Cordoba in Spain where it originates, Victoria in Australia or from Chile. Different continents, hemispheres and growing conditions. The hojiblanca extra virgin olive oil is generally medium to robust in intensity and the flavours on the palate are complex with many layers of fruitiness, bitterness and pepperiness, the three positive flavour characteristics. The pepperiness in hojiblanca starts at the back of the palate and throat and flows in waves over the entire palate with warmth and spiciness reminiscent of a mouthful of a mixture of chilli, pepper and a bitter spicy vegetable such as cress or arugula. The spiciness is persistent and the nuance which helps me distinguish this varietal from all the others which produce a similarly bitter spicy oil is a late chilli tingling sensation on the front of the tongue and palate. Along with the aroma, general intensity and flavours of the oil this is an example of the distinguishing feature which experienced tasters use to identify the oils from different varietals. The taster who achieved a perfect score in the Savante Skills Test has an encyclopaedic memory of these markers for the different varietal oils she tastes, hence the perfect identification of the eight different varietal oils from eight different regions presented in the test.

In the continuing development of the Savantes tasting philosophy we have developed the concept of 'The Palette of Flavours' with colours representing the positive characteristics of fruitiness (blue), bitterness (green) and spiciness (red). To represent the progression of flavours along the palate, a graph has been devised with the vertical axis representing intensity and the horizontal axis representing time in one second intervals. By tasting the extra virgin olive oil three times – concentrating on one characteristic each time – a visual representation of the intensities and length of each can be developed. The resulting 'Savantes Savourgram©' gives an excellent display of the comparative intensities and persistence of fruitiness, bitterness and spiciness. The balance, complexity, harmony and persistence can be assessed by looking at the Savourgram©. The representation adds another dimension, that of time.

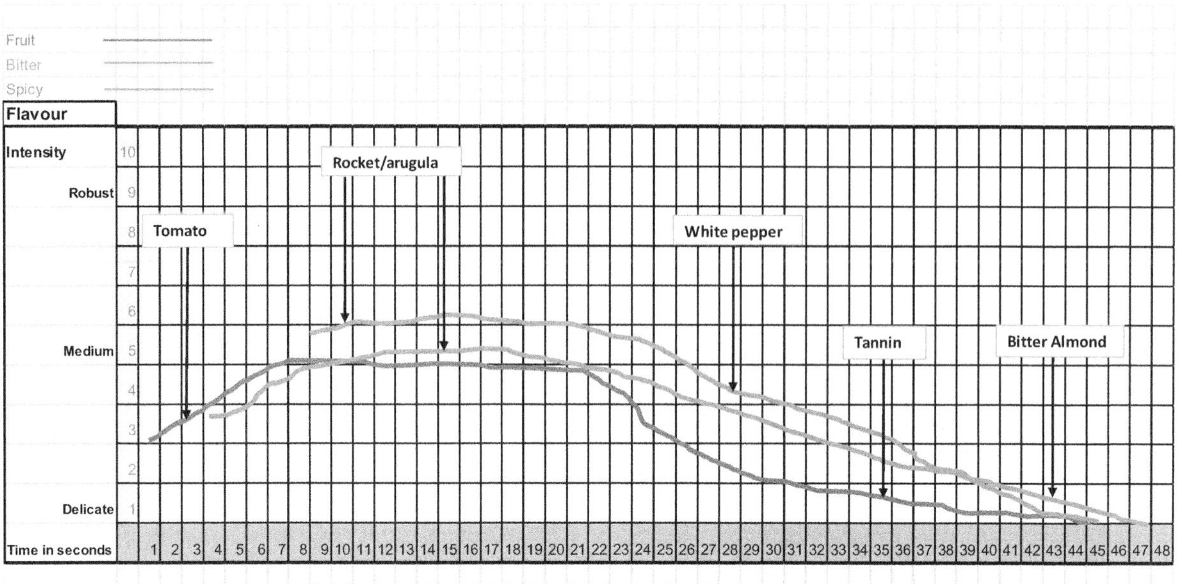

A Sample Savantes Savourgram©

The addition of the fruits, vegetal, spicy and nutty food ingredient flavours detected, and where on the palate they occur, completes an evocative picture for the consumer of the oil.

The process is a practical visual way to compare the assessment of oils between tasters and to represent the aroma and flavour profile to consumers on websites. The Savourgram© provides a visual tool to introduce consumers to the positive flavour characteristics of a range of extra virgin olive oils. It will also assist in the blending of oils to achieve a particular flavour profile.

Regarding flavour 'groups', the alert reader will notice the switching between the descriptors used to describe the perceived 'heat' of extra virgin olive oils. We have searched for an evocative descriptor having rejected the 'pungency' used by some institutions as too closely associated with chemicals. The prosaic 'heat' may suggest the oil has been burnt by using excessive heat during extraction – a ploy used to extract more oil. We have interchanged pepperiness and spiciness and tried to use them when the flavours relate to pepper or other spices. However, these do not describe the heat in arugula or rocket, or wasabi which are not spices or peppery. Recently we have come across the descriptor 'fieriness' and will test this more generic term amongst tasters to see if it is acceptable.

An important motivation in these developments has been to prove that an entire learning system which links knowledge to productive commercial activities can be developed by a producer without the support and limitations of government institutions and the compromises and conformity in delivery which this support necessitates.

Standardisation Blunts Innovation

The olive oil industry is beset by government and institutional intervention and inducements which act like a straitjacket curtailing exploration, innovation and progression. There is a culture of dependency which has developed over generations and is sustained by grants and subsidies. It seems the customer is no longer the consumer, who has been replaced by the providers of financial support, status and favourable legislation. The pace of change in the conservative institutions of this very traditional and highly politicised agrarian industry is pedestrian.

The competitiveness of our product depends on innovation and a diversity of approaches, not centralised control and standardisation. There are many ways in which producers can promote and effect change, the platform for this is the confidence a profound knowledge of the product and market imparts. Lack of knowledge renders the producers impotent in affecting decisions which have an impact on their livelihood. Distance from the consumer caused by the many steps in the supply chain makes the producer vulnerable to being subverted by the interests of those who profit along the way. Sometimes this is the situation preferred by those in positions of power to minimise the potency of movements advancing the interests of farmers.

Standardisation is a word commonly used in the global olive oil industry. While some degree of standardisation is necessary for the integrity of some processes such as classification of olive oil by organoleptic or tasting panels and tasting competency of individuals, diversity in other aspects of the industry such as training and styles of extra virgin olive oil will strengthen the base. The predictability and rigidity of centralisation and standardisation will make the industry vulnerable to competing interests.

An important consequence of acquiring authoritative knowledge is the ability to take to task those who work on the periphery of the supply chain with self-proclaimed expertise. Posts on social media from these individuals making judgements on products which have an impact on the livelihood of other individuals must be called to account. The industry needs a coherent competency-based recognition system for an individual's tasting competency and associated adherence to a code of ethics covering commentary on the quality of extra virgin olive oils. This system will go beyond technical sensory training, covering aroma and taste, to include the impact that sight and emotion have in persuading consumers to consume more olive oil. It need not be centrally administered by another bureaucracy, rather a set of clearly articulated activities and results which training and communication enterprises espouse.

Savantes is a movement initiated to show that a producer can directly affect change. Not everyone has the desire to become so immersed in the downstream industry and will choose to access less time-consuming paths. There are many other offerings of taste training ranging from the technical training to become a member of a panel to short courses of a day or so. When choosing a course, it is suggested that self-promoting accolades of expertise after a short course should be shunned. Choose an international programme which emphasises the market within which all the tasting activities must operate. Choose practical tasting over technical tasting if your main interest is sales rather than olive oil classification. Having mastered the profiling of a range of olive oils from around the world, make the effort to understand the use of olive oil as an ingredient in the food of many nations. Engage with the consumer. In most cities on all continents there is an eclectic selection of cuisines which are potential consumers – European, North American, South American, Asian, African, Middle Eastern – which have preferences for different styles and origins of extra virgin olive oil. The whole palette of taste combinations and ingredients will open for your enjoyment.

A World of Flavours

Following pursuit of knowledge about a product, and perhaps in parallel, the understanding of the politics of the marketplace is an asset. The politics of the olive oil industry has its seat in the history and regions of the producing countries.

There are tomes written on the association of the olive trees with human movement from Asia Minor to the Mediterranean Basin and from there around the world. The stories will not be repeated here as we are dealing with the contemporary olive oil industry where history explains why different regions and populations behave in differing ways.

The Origin of The Olive Tree

Reading the history written by historians and their acolytes, one is led to believe that the olive tree originated in the Eastern Mediterranean basin, spreading from there to cover all the countries which surround the Mediterranean Sea. There are many claims as to the origin of the olive within this area with records of ancient trees staking a claim to be the oldest. There is a delightful book written about the oldest olive tree titled 'The Angel Tree: The Enchanting Quest for the World's Oldest Olive Tree' by Alex Dingwall-Main. The story is told of the commissioning of a distinguished landscape artist by a wealthy Frenchman in Provence to find the oldest olive tree in the world to be transplanted for the centrepiece in the garden of his recently renovated mansion. The book describes the human and botanical landscape surrounding the olive tree far better than a few paragraphs here.

There is a possible counter claim to the world's origin of the olive tree which comes from Asia Minor, reputed to be the original source of the olive which was transported to the Mediterranean Basin and selectively bred to produce the Olea europaea which populates the main producing regions. Studies of the genetics of the African olive, taxonomically variously described as Olea europaea subspecies cuspidata or Olea africana, found throughout Asia and Africa may be the precursor of the European olive. Could the olive we know so well be Olea africana – sub-species europaea? An analysis done at the University of Haripur by Hussain et al suggests that the olives may have common ancestry with the selected quote from the abstract of their paper published in 2017. [1]

My research in the Cape Province of South Africa suggests that the African olive, which is common in the region, was used by the Venda and early settling tribes for medicinal and cultural purposes long before the European settlers brought the European olive and established it in groves in the Cape. As in Kashmir it is common practice to graft the European olive tree onto the rootstock of the African olive.

Notwithstanding this interesting exploration of origins, where the European tree originates in the Mediterranean is of little consequence as the selective breeding produces new varietals and the originals continue to be the main source of olive oil production in the older established regions.

Touring the Olive Regions

The best way to find out about the different approaches and nuances of olive oil producers and traders is to travel. If you live in Europe this is relatively easy through brief forays into selected countries. Those who live on other continents must make a greater effort and be more selective about the destination to get maximum return from time invested.

The countries which show the biggest contrast in their approach to production and organisation of their industries are Spain and Italy. With some exceptions, Spain is organised into large cooperatives or companies producing substantial volumes of all classifications of olive oil. Italy's production and marketing is less cohesive with many small groves clustered around villages producing a small volume of estate extra virgin olive oil with sales often linked to agritourism.

---

[1] ' Hussain et al.: Genetic relationship analysis of wild and cultivated olive-Abstract. Wild (O. cuspidata) and cultivated olive (O. europaea) grow in northern regions of Pakistan including Azad Jammu and Kashmir are expected to have considerable inter and intra-species genetic variability due to adaptation to the various environmental conditions. The genetic relationship was investigated in wild and cultivated olive populations growing in Azad Jammu and Kashmir .... Four clusters were clearly separating wild and cultivated olive populations from each other indicated that the Olea cuspidata (wild) which is an Afro-Asiatic species found particularly in this region and Olea europaea (cultivated) were divergent. The insightful difference between wild and cultivated populations and the close relationship among Olea europaea accessions had confirmed that the cultivated olive did not develop locally but were introduced from abroad, propagated by grafting on local wild olive. Moreover, analysis of cultivated olive showed that they are probably from same population with common ancestry.'

Spain with its dominance in the production of olive oil has a substantial influence over the global olive oil trading environment and strategic decisions made by the authorities have a great impact on trading and the well-being of producers. In 2020, with the imminent oversupply of olive oil, the Spanish government and some industry leaders were advocating earlier harvesting to produce higher quality extra virgin olive oil and reduce the oil yield. This is nonsensical if you believe that the price increase caused by spreading the cost of production over a smaller volume and the more robust flavour profile are two factors limiting the increased use of extra virgin olive oil by consumers. Taking action to reduce the price and flavour intensity may result in a greater volume of oil being produced and the consumption increasing.

In 2022 there will be a significant reduction in production in Spain, Italy, Greece and France which suggests that later harvesting with higher volumes may be a viable option.

Spain

Spain produces the full range of classifications with over 40% of production coming from the southern region of Andalucia. Traditional varieties grown here are picual, hojiblanca, and picuda. These generally produce robust bitter, spicy or peppery extra virgin olive oils. There are many Denomination of Origin Boards (PDO's) which oversee and certify the quality of the locally produced extra virgin olive oil. The activities of the PDO's vary, with some having well trained tasting panels to ensure the conformity of the oils to trade standards. Priego de Cordoba has a very influential PDO which encourages a very high quality with an outstanding record for varietals and blends of hojiblanca and picuda winning the top prizes in many competitions worldwide. Another notable region is Baena, both are worth visiting.

The city of Priego de Cordoba is an excellent example of an olive oil city. Taking great pride in their reputation as producers of high quality extra virgin olive oil and recognising the employment this provides, the people of Priego de Cordoba take every opportunity to promote local products. Local brands in abundance are on the tables of restaurants and hotel dining rooms with the proprietors ready to discuss their merits. One expects that if a defective or sub-standard olive oil was presented in this city, word would get around very quickly and it would disappear with the brand reputation damaged.

Andalucia is worth visiting to enjoy the delights of Seville and Cordoba as well as the surrounding olive producing regions. Other local varieties which produce excellent oils to savour are manzanilla and those which are more recent plantings from northern regions, the ubiquitous arbequina and the robust oil producing cornicabra. Arbequina dominates the northern region of Catalunya. The oils from this variety are less robust than those of the south and more suited to coastal cuisine which uses a lot of fish. The arbequina tree is versatile growing in a range of environments including super high-density configurations. As a result, it is found in many regions and countries, including Greece and the Southern Hemisphere in general.

To continue with our tour of Spain during which you will be experiencing the culture, the life, the music, the tastes, the attitudes and the extra virgin olive oils associated with each locality and region to give you a substantial compendium. It is this blend of people and product which is the heart of extra virgin olive oil. In the twenty years of presenting Extra Virgin Olive Oil Savantes, probably the greatest compliment paid to our approach came from a prominent producer of award-winning high quality extra virgin olive oil from Cordoba in Andalucia who said, 'The course surprised me very much. It is way more advanced than any other course that I went to in the past. I mention "advanced" meaning that you see olive oil from a higher perspective than a regular technical course. You learn how to love olive oil from the heart of the olive oil.'

It is the association with culture which sets olive oil apart from the broadacre produced vegetable oils like canola and soybean oil. A differentiation which may well be undermined by the modern trend towards olive oil production from super high-density groves.

Other varieties which can be explored in Spain are less common and some are confined to specific localities with a particular microclimate. Cornicabra is grown in Castilla La Mancha where the historic city of Toledo is well worth visiting. This varietal can now be found in other regions where olive oil production is expanding such as Extramadura where the historic Roman town of Merida is worth a stopover. Alfafarenca can be found in Valencia and Alicante provinces along with blanqueta. Both these produce extra virgin olive oils which tend to be delicate to medium or 'sweeter' than the bitter Andalusian oils, perhaps a result of the proximity to the coast and fish with its relatively delicate tastes being a common food. A more robust oil found in small quantities from these provinces is changlot real. Empeltre produces an oil of delicate and subtle tastes and is found mainly up north of Spain in Aragon, the olives also produce an excellent flavoursome naturally fermented black table olive. Granada is a famed historic city, and the surrounds are home to the lechin variety which is also found in adjacent provinces. As with many Spanish varieties there are 'sub' varieties named after the regions, for example lechin de Granada, lechin de Sevilla, manzanilla Cacerena, manzanilla de Sevilla.

There are many other lesser known varieties which have relatively small areas devoted to them with the quantity of oil produced limiting availability to small product lines mainly available in boutique olive oil shops. Occasionally there are seminars or tastings held which explore the lesser varietals, some of which are being reintroduced as producers look to differentiate their products from the mainstream varietal oils.

France

From northern eastern Spain one can cross the border into France and experience the flavoursome and different extra virgin olive oils of Provence. Generally, the varietals are specific to the region and not found grown in other countries, except for picholine which is grown in Australasia, the USA, Morocco and elsewhere. Frantoio, the Italian varietal, and the Spanish arbequina are new arrivals to add to the range of cultivars grown by some boutique olive producers. The main French varietals are l'aglandau which produces an attractive and particularly nutty extra virgin olive oil which tasters who are not familiar with the flavour may deem to be rancid. Other varieties are bouteillan, grossane, picholine, salonenque, and tanche. Produced in small volumes the Provencal olive oils are rarely available outside France. The dual purpose varieties, tanche, salonenque, grossane and picholine tend to produce delicate to medium oils. They are generally blended with more robust l'aglandau and earlier harvested oils. The flavours of the oils are herbal, vegetal and nutty. Interesting, unusual aromas include lavender, presumably from the groves where lavender is interplanted between the trees. Dill also grows as a weed in some groves and often the aroma of this herb can be detected in the oils.

Olive oil has historically been used as a carrier in perfumes and aromatic body lotions due to its ability to absorb the chemical compounds which impart specific aromas. It is common to detect aromas in the oil which reflect the herbs or other plants which populate the grove or the surrounds. Examples are camomile in Greece, eucalyptus in Australia, and as mentioned, lavender in France.

Observers and participants in tasting courses are sometimes befuddled by the array of aromas and flavours experienced tasters detect and describe in olive oils. This often leads to some scepticism about the whole flavour description.

However, the aromas and tastes of fruit, vegetables, herbs and spices are attributable to many chemical compounds which plants synthesise from the nutrient inputs. The banana aromas in some extra virgin olive oils are produced from the same compound that produces them in bananas, 3-methylbutyl acetate. Ethyl propanoate and hexanal can give the apple aroma and flavour. How these compounds express themselves in an olive oil depends on their concentration and the presence of other compounds with which they react. Hence when blending one does not necessarily get the linear sum of the flavours of the oils to be blended, the result is a new oil where the flavours are the sum of the reactions of the ingredients. If a new blend is left for a few days, its flavour profile will change as reactions continue until the oil has 'settled'. Not recognising this has sometimes led to a sample taken immediately after blending and sent to a customer differing from the oil which is then delivered a short time later. Another occasion when this may occur is when blending by pumping one oil into the storage tank followed by another without agitating the final mix. Being of different specific gravities the oils tend to settle in layers. If a sample is taken from the bottom of the tank and sent to the customer, it is likely to differ from the oil later despatched when mixing takes place during the process of emptying the tank into a tanker for delivery.

Back to France where the extra virgin olive oils are different and well worth exploring. Not surprisingly some of the aromas are reminiscent of the mixture of dry herbs or 'Herbs de Provence' which grace many spice racks around the world. Much of the French cuisine is butter-based and does not seem to have evolved around olive oil as it has in the major producing countries. The influx of migrants from the former French colonies of Tunisia and Algeria, both olive oil consuming regions, has increased the use of extra virgin olive oil, especially in the cuisine of the coastal cities and ports such as Marseille.

There is one notable product produced in Provence which is unique. It is fermented olive oil which is classified as virgin olive oil and goes under various names such as 'fruite noir' or black fruit as in very ripe late harvested olives. The olives are purposely fermented after harvest prior to the oil being extracted. The product has a unique and acquired taste and often costs more than extra virgin olive oil. Aficionados may frown on the 'defective' olive oil offered for sale; however, it has a market and is legitimised by its use in the cuisine of the region and properly labelled and identified. It is a good example of differentiation which challenges the industry mantra which strives to produce a more and more standardised style of extra virgin olive oil worldwide.

Italy

The next destination in our travels across the northern Mediterranean is the province of Liguria in Italy which surrounds the historic port city of Genoa. The taggiasca olive variety grows on the picturesque, terraced hills and produces a delicate oil with subtle aromas. As mentioned earlier, the low level of antioxidants means the product has a limited shelf-life of around a year if stored correctly. Ideally suited to the fish cuisine, which is offered along the coast, the subtle tastes of this 'sweet' oil are a contrast to the bold robust flavours of so many olive oils. Detecting and describing the flavours of oils takes practice and an open mind. Too often inexperienced tasters dismiss these delicate and subtle oils as flavourless, oxidised, refined, even rancid as their senses struggle to savour the very delicate aromas and flavours. The approach to tasting should always be that the olive oil is likely to be extra virgin until proven otherwise, the olive oil justice system – 'extra virgin until proven defective'. These delicate oils should be protected from the push for more robust olive oils which tend to be in favour with tasting panels from other regions and competition judging panels. In any tasting session they should be tasted first, tasting them after robust oils will numb the palate to their subtlety.

Most of the olive oil from Italy comes from the southern regions, approximately 60% from Puglia and Calabria and 11% from Sicily. The northern provinces are relatively small producers by volume with the central provinces of Lazio, Tuscany, Umbria and Abruzzo producing about 11% of Italy's olive oil. The production in the north and central regions is generally from small groves, often linked to agritourism which provides an important market for the extra virgin olive oils. There are some varieties which are found in many groves in particular regions and there are some which are specific to towns and surrounding areas, often overseen by a Denomination of Origin authority controlling style and quality. The varieties frantoio, moraiolo, leccino and pendolino are found in abundance in central Italy and are often combined in a fruity blend of medium intensity. An example of a local varietal is olivastra seggianese which is grown around the town of Seggiano. The picturesque town is notable for another interesting olive tree phenomenon. Suspended high in a 200-year-old cistern is an olive tree with its roots bared so that any communication can be detected and measured. Known as 'Olivo del Cisterone', the olivastra seggianese tree is grown aeroponically and is reputed to communicate via its roots.

Heading further south, a stopover in Modena is recommended, not necessarily for its olive oil, for all the other things this genteel city is famous for. Non-culinary attractions are the Ferraris, Ducatis and Maseratis and other famous motorcar and motorcycle brands which come from here. Then there is Luciano Pavarotti, the world famous and much-loved operatic tenor who came from Modena. The Mercato Albinelli food and vegetable market in central Modena with its centrepiece fountain of the woman with her shopping basket is one of the best markets I have visited. It provides a visual reference for many vegetables, an extraordinary range of tomatoes and salad vegetables, fruit, nuts, herbs, spices – everything. The region is also the home of parmigiano reggiano and many of the stalls in the market offer various brands.

Traditional balsamic vinegar, the real Aceto Balsamico Tradizionale aged for a minimum of 12 years, comes from the attics of many homes in Modena. Made from the must of Trebbiano and or Lambrusco grapes the mother barrel containing the 'family's' special fermentation ingredients is given to the daughter when she marries. Traditionally the making of the balsamic is the domain of the women who oversee the aging process through evaporative concentration in a set of five barrels decreasing in size. Balsamic tasting is as complex as tasting olive oil and is well worth experiencing. Parma ham comes from Parma just north-west of Modena where you can also enjoy opera at Teatro Regio di Parma. South-west is Bologna, a city of historical significance with another wonderful food culture and market. The University of Bologna is reputed to be the world's first university. Where else in the world can you find such an indulgence of luxurious sensorial experiences – definitely worth taking a few days out of your olive oil exploration.

Travelling south you will reach Puglia with the port city of Bari being the technical centre of the Italian olive industry. Here the groves are larger and populated by coratina which produces a robust oil. The variety is now found in the southern hemisphere and produces consistently high quality complex oil. Other varieties found in Puglia are ogliarola, peranzana and the newer FS17 or favalosa. Calabria further south also produces large quantities of olive oil from the coratina, carolea and ottobratica varieties. Calabrese brands are not as prominent in the world market as those from other Italian regions.

Sicily produces some high quality and complex extra virgin olive oils in small to medium size groves. An interesting region which through centuries has been occupied by many invaders, the rugged island has an eclectic vegetation fare, and produces wines and tree crops of world renown. The main olive oil varieties are nocellara del belice, biancolilla, and cerasuolo which are retailed as varietals and blends of all three. There are some localised varieties such as tonda iblea which in my opinion is the best match with a caprese salad of tasty tomato, fresh buffalo mozzarella, basil, a sprinkle of sea salt liberally drizzled with extra virgin tonda iblea olive oil. Aromatic, mouth-watering and so healthy.

A tip here on the adding of olive oil to salad. The oil acts as a barrier and stops ingredients from mixing with the salad vegetables. The trick is to mix all the ingredients such as salad leaves, sea salt, pepper, lemon juice, balsamic vinegar first, then add the olive oil and toss the salad again. If the olive oil, vinegar, lemon and condiments are mixed first and then tossed in the salad, the olive oil will stop the other ingredients contacting the vegetables. The general rule is to add the extra virgin olive oil last.

The islands of Corsica and Sardinia, respectively part of France and Italy, also produce extra virgin olive oils of note. The varieties are local and the volumes small and not often found in mainstream retail. They can be obtained from reputable international online stores.

Greece

Across the Ionian Sea to the west of southern Italy is the world's highest olive oil consuming country, Greece. In 2008 the per capita consumption of olive oil in Greece was just above 20kg, compared with around 10kg per person in Spain and Italy. In the ten-year period to 2018 the consumption in Greece halved to 10kg then increased to around 12.5kg. The trend in Spain and Italy is also down ending up just below 10kg per capita in 2018. There are many theories proffered to explain this decline, the most common is the loss of disposable income across the entire population following the decline in the national economy. There is also the possibility that the prevalent Mediterranean diet has lost ground to the western fast-food culture popular amongst the younger consumers.

The two main olive oil producing areas in Greece are the Peloponnese and Crete. The main varieties are kalamon, which is mainly cultivated to produce the famed kalamata olives, and koroneiki from which the vast majority of Greek olive oil is produced. The olive groves carpet entire valleys, and the farms are generally small. There are some large corporations which aggregate the oil from small producers into international brands, however, many of the producers take their product to the market. Coming mainly from the one variety, Greek olive oils are similar and lack variation. The differentiation mainly comes from harvest timing and subtle differences in microclimates and vegetation. The extra virgin olive oils are generally delicate to medium with subtle tastes, often with flavours of the many herbs like oregano and thyme which grow wild in the grove. The flavours of the oils are well suited to the mainly fish diet. The farmers' markets offer a range of wild vegetables, such as the sweet wild asparagus, which present new additions for the taster's aroma and taste vocabulary. The marketing of the oils would benefit from the use of these flavour descriptions to build the mystique of Greek cuisine and associated extra virgin olive oils.

Crete also produces a large volume of olive oil, again mainly from the koroneiki variety.

In a search for differentiated Greek oils to present to the world through Savantes a few oils from different varieties have been tasted, namely tsounati and makri. There are different varieties on the islands but few of them seem to be available outside Greece. The industry would be well served to differentiate their olive oils and offer a wider variety of flavours. This may be difficult as the different varieties are interplanted in the ancient groves and identification for separate harvesting will take some effort. This effort may well be rewarded with high prices.

An olive mill near Sparta late in the harvesting season presented a memorable experience for the hospitality and the opportunity to taste fresh extra virgin olive oil. The mill in question has two extraction lines using a three-phase and two-phase system of separation. The phases refer to the residue or pomace left after the oil has been extracted. Each line washes the olives which are then crushed to a paste before being mixed in a malaxer to help separate the oil from the solids. A centrifuge then separates the oil which is pumped off into storage tanks. Two-phase leaves a wet pomace containing the water and solid matter from the olive, three phase leaves a drier pomace and vegetable water. We had the rare opportunity to taste the fresh extra virgin olive oil from the same olives put through each of these systems and compare their flavour profile with the oil which floated to the surface in the mixer phase or malaxer before going through the centrifuges or decanters. This oil which aggregates on the surface is a called afforiato (what comes to the surface) in Italy and the sinolea system is designed to extract it using rotating discs.

There was discernible difference in the flavour profile of the three olive oils with the most robust and complex being the oil from the malaxers, followed by the oil from the two-phase system with the three-phase system producing a less complex and less robust oil. The underlying flavours were the same in the three samples, however the intensity was discernibly different. This is expected as the three-phase system uses more added water than the two-phase system. The biophenols, or polyphenols, which impart the flavour in extra virgin olive oils are soluble in water and more will be removed with the higher water requirement. This is a valuable demonstration on the importance of choosing the most suitable extraction system from the many that are available from brands engineered and manufactured in many countries. Furthermore, the technology is always evolving and improving, necessitating continuing research by producers to select equipment or the best toll processors. The miller is as important as the equipment, master millers can extract the best from an olive oil where an inexperienced miller may well make a lower quality olive oil from good quality olives.

While in the Spartan mill I experienced an incident symptomatic of the homogeneity of Greek olive oils. Tasting the fresh oils as they were extracted, a farmer brought in a fresh oil from the local athinolia variety. It was quite different from the koroneiki oils coming out of the mill from previous batches. The flavours were fruity, even citrus, with a pleasant nutty finish. Commenting to the millers on the differentiation of the oil and the potential market for this different style at higher price than the ubiquitous koroneiki, the writer was admonished as the farmer would demand a higher price. Later in the evening when the time came for the farmer to be paid, he referenced my comments on his oil and asked for a higher price. His request was met with the offer to take the standard price or take the oil. The farmer relented and the oil went into the tank with all the other oils and the opportunity was missed. Another oil which can add fruitiness to a blend or be presented as a varietal from the Peloponnese region is that from the manaki variety.

The day in the mill turned into one of the most memorable experiences in twenty years of involvement with the olive industry. After the last batch of olives was processed late into the evening, the brothers who owned the business prepared a meal in the small kitchen. There was abundant fresh seafood, risotto, spanakopita or spinach pie made by the grandmother, salads with vegetables from the garden outside the mill and wild asparagus from under the olive trees. Vegetables were grilled on an olive wood fired brazier outside. The food covered the table and was liberally drizzled with extra virgin olive oil extracted that day. Home-made red wine filled the glasses and soon emptied, at the end of the meal home-made tsiporou was sipped and small Greek cigars enjoyed in moderation. There was no other moderation about this very special treat, it was pinnacle of Greek hospitality and food with simplicity and humility. If only it could be bottled!

In the continuing effort to spread the knowledge of olive oils from other regions a bottle of Sicilian extra virgin olive oil blended from the nocellara del belice, cerasuolo and biancolillo varieties had been presented to the owners. Surreptitiously, halfway through dinner the oldest brother picked the bottle up from under the table and drizzled the oil on his salad. A compliment to the excellence of the Sicilian oil, the move was noticed, and inappropriate comments were made about a Greek enjoying an Italian olive oil, with laughter all around. Earlier in the afternoon an impromptu tasting of some Spanish and Italian oils had been held in the offices. The robust Spanish oils did not suit the palates of the producers and would not have paired well with the delicate flavours of the fare to be offered that night.

It is experiences like this which are the soul of involvement in the olive industry and occur serendipitously. They are not available in travel brochures. Conferences and haughty tasting sessions do not represent or capture the essence of the industry which flows through the groves and the veins of the producers. Far removed from those whose livelihood they are affecting, bureaucrats and politicians make decisions which do not consider the impact on the daily lives of those in the groves. Somehow, this lifestyle must be preserved while the demands of modernity and ever evolving technology are satisfied. Some say the ancient olive and its remarkable association with mankind over centuries imparts a right to the respect of olive oil and profitable returns to producers which are well above production costs. This is not the way of the world driven by competition and a hunger for growth and largesse. Olive oil is considered a staple in the Mediterranean and is often used as a loss leader, like milk and bread, to attract custom to retailers. Intellectuals in ivory towers decry this practice as not being worthy of such an adored product. Their outrage will not stop the drive for increased efficiency which is spawning super high-density production where the olive tree is just one of a million bushes in a hedge which is mechanically managed and remotely controlled.

It is paradoxical that the mystique of olive oil produced and sold from these super groves is derived from the stories built around centuries old, gnarled trees which stand proud on their own. The industry seems to be caught between preserving the tradition surrounding olive oil and the drive to commoditise it to gain more profit. Can governments continue to subsidise groves which sustain local communities and provide destinations for tourists and their full wallets? There is no easy resolution for this continuing tension between ancient and modern. Resolving it becomes more difficult the further apart the two cultures and associated aspirations become. However, the olive tree has so often in the past asserted itself in moderating extremes of expectation manifest in its manipulation by humans. Sitting in a tobacco smoke-stained hotel room in Sparta in the early hours of the morning after the feast in the mill there is a feeling that time and distance will create two worlds, that of the traditional producer of olive oil with their acolytes and the modern corporate producers for which price and stockturns are the driver.

After the magical experience in the Peloponnese, northern Greece around Thessaloniki presents a different perspective with the dominance of table olive production, especially large green ones. Olive oil from this region often comes from table varieties which are lower in polyphenols and produce a delicate creamy oil.

My host for a visit to this region was a world-renowned professor and author whose life was the study of olive oil. Generously giving his time to show me the history and ancient culture of the region, the genial professor took me to The Museum of the Royal Tombs at Aigai and to many, many churches of historical consequence. Eventually, with my ecclesiastical senses saturated by the second day he asked if I would like to see more churches, and if not, what would I like to do. 'Eat Greek food' was my quick response. We went to a taverna at a little fishing port and from midday to the evening our hosts brought dish after dish of seafood and vegetables. The afternoon was whiled away with conversation about Greek culture, food, olive oil and any other topic that came to mind. This was more akin to my church, while respecting those who are devout.

The island of Crete is Greece's largest exporter of extra virgin olive oil, most of which comes from the koroneiki variety. There are some local varieties of which tsounati is one.

Adriatic

North of Greece are the countries of the Adriatic all of which produce olive oil in varying quantities, little of which is exported and available outside the respective country. Croatian and Slovenian oils feature well in international competitions and come from varieties such as busa, oblica and bianchera which are unique to the region. The oils vary in intensity with most being fruity and medium to delicate, suiting the fish-based diet of the coastal regions. Like producers who in the past have concentrated on developing their product in the local market, some are taking the significant step to exporting their brands. One essential of supply to retail which must be delivered is consistency, both product and supply. Vendors get upset when they build a story around and promote a new product only to find that the supply runs out, the flavour profile fluctuates and the price changes. Experience with some suppliers reveals difficulty in meeting this criterion, especially continuity of supply. Often in the sheer delight following successfully placing a product in several outlets the oil runs out and the shelf-space is permanently lost to a competitor. It is better to start small, thereby ensuring supply to a few buyers.

Turkey

East across the Aegean Sea, Turkey produces large volumes of olive oil, much of which is sold in bulk. As in the Adriatic countries, olive production thrives along the coast and producers are moving to brand their extra virgin olive oil for sale into the high-end international market. The varieties are mostly local with ayvalik or edremit dominating the north and memecik in the south. Turkey is a large producer of table olives and many of the varieties are dual purpose with the olives not used for pickling being processed to oil. The result is that the oils are generally fruity and delicate to medium intensity. The presence of branded bottles of Turkish extra virgin olive oils at international food fairs is increasing and offers a good opportunity to explore the flavours. As the export market evolves and the oils from this country are more differentiated, they will increase their share of the high-end market. Currently the lower price for their oils, as with Tunisia and other emerging producing countries, reflects the availability of large volumes of oil with similar flavour and chemical profiles, and a lack of a range of intensities and flavours.

North Africa

Tunisia has become one of the top four olive oil producing countries, regularly competing with Greece and Italy for the second and third highest production behind Spain. The main variety in Tunisia is chemlali, which with chetoui makes up over 90% of the country's olive population. While there are some excellent Tunisian extra virgin olive oils which do well in international competitions of note, generally the dominance of two varieties results in olive oils of similar profiles with little differentiation other than that which can be achieved from varying intensity through harvest timing.

The flavour profile of bulk extra virgin olive oils from koroneiki in Greece, the main Turkish varieties and chemlali and chetoui from Tunisia are generally similar and delicate to medium intensity. The massively increased production from Tunisia will challenge the place of bulk Greek oils which hitherto have been bought at relatively low prices for blending with Italian and Spanish oils. The tariffs placed on Spanish oils in the USA has already seen a substantial increase in Tunisian oil imported into the USA in blends retailed by some of the major brands. This surge will also make it difficult for olive oils from Turkey to make rapid inroads into the market for lower priced blending oils. The demand for Tunisian extra virgin olive oil can be expected to decline when the USA removes the tariffs imposed as the result of World Trade Organisation ruling on the European Union's subsidies to Airbus. However, many of the new contacts made with Tunisian producers will persist after the removal of the punitive tariffs on Spanish oil and the replacement of Greek olive oils with Tunisian production will continue.

It came as a surprise to find the lack of interest from a Greek panel in tasting olive oils from Tunisia. It was apparent that Tunisian oils had not been tasted at all. Not only is it important to understand and monitor competing products so one can manoeuvre to present one's own product as an alternative, there is also a commercial opportunity to offer classification tasting services to Tunisia and Turkey for their oils which regularly have problems with classification by Spanish panels which are used to tasting more robust styles of extra virgin olive oil.

Morocco is a country which produces some brands of high-end extra virgin olive oil. Large modern intensive groves have been planted by Spanish interests and much of the oil is used to supplement Spanish production. The varieties planted are Spanish. Some local varieties dominated by picholine marocaine and some of its clonal selections are used for olive oil and table olives.

Asia

To complete our tour of the northern hemisphere, new plantings in sub-continental Asian countries Pakistan, India and Bangladesh must be acknowledged. When established with relatively inexpensive labour these countries can be expected to produce large volumes of bulk extra virgin olive oils from imported Spanish and Italian varieties. The benefit of this will be a foothold in these countries to build a following for the use of olive oil and replace the vegetable oils currently used.

The same can be said for China which has won its first awards for extra virgin olive oil in international competitions and has exported its first olive oil to a neighbouring country. China has the capacity to rapidly expand its industry with low production costs to produce bulk oils which will compete in international trade with Turkish, Greek and Tunisian exports. These countries will be well advised to monitor the developments of the olive industry to their east and develop contingency plans for their own production. The oils produced by China will most likely come from the major European varieties which were planted as long as 20 years ago in experimental plots. Chinese conglomerates own some significant and well-established European brands which may well become the vehicle for the entry of Chinese olive oil into the mainstream market.

Declining consumption in Mediterranean countries and tariffs limiting consumption in major importing countries such as the USA has forced the main exporting countries in the European Union to seek markets in Asian countries, especially China. It is possible that the growth in olive oil consumption in Asia will be driven by domestic production and not imports.

Japan imports large volumes of extra virgin olive oil for its discerning consumers. There is a small domestic production on Shodoshima Island which presents several competition winning brands for the more affluent Japanese customer. From first production in 1908, two prefectures cultivated olives up to 2006, increasing to 16 prefectures in the next ten years. Olive oil production in Japan is on the march.

Old World and New World

For ease of reference, olive oil producing countries are roughly categorised as 'old world' covering the traditional olive growing countries of the Mediterranean and 'new world' covering the developing production in the southern hemisphere as well as the Asian countries and the USA in the northern hemisphere.

The USA is the largest importer of olive oil outside the European Union. In California there has been olive oil production since the 1800's from olives brought over by the clergy from Spain. Cultivars were selected from groves of these trees to establish large commercial enterprises and the name 'mission' was selected for the variety. A century later, unable to compete with the olive oil imported from the Mediterranean countries, production switched to table olives with the development of the 'California black-ripe' curing method using lye treatment and oxygenation. Canned black olives became the main product line and olive oil was produced from the olives unsuitable for canning. Disease and competition slowly diminished the table olive industry and in the last decade of the twentieth century planting of high-density and super high-density groves began. The varieties planted in these and medium-density groves in this new surge represent most of the main varieties available in the Mediterranean regions of Spain, Italy and Greece. The table olive groves have mainly been replaced with almond and citrus orchards; however, some groves of mission remain and produce extra virgin olive oil.

New groves are being planted in other states, Florida, Oregon, Georgia, Texas and Arizona. This enthusiasm for olive oil production is ignited by entrepreneurs who establish nurseries and new systems to supply receptive investors seduced by the charisma of the olive tree and associated visions of profits from import replacement. The 'new world' producing countries – USA, New Zealand, Australia, Argentina, Chile, Uruguay, Peru, Brazil, Mexico, South Africa and Namibia – have all been through, or are going through, this cycle. In some countries the tide is ebbing, in others such as the USA it is on the rise.

The varieties planted in the new producing countries, with few exceptions such as the arauco or azapa in Argentina and Chile, mission in South Africa and corregiolo in Australia, are mainstream Mediterranean varieties. The olive oils produced are generally of a high standard and little refining is undertaken. The flavours can be similar to their northern hemisphere counterparts and feed into the trading system for these oils. In some microclimates the oils produced differ in flavour from those produced in Spain, Greece and Italy.

With the new high-density plantings around the world, particular varieties are starting to dominate the supply – arbequina is an example. This will move olive oil towards a commodity and while the hope of investors may be to attract the high prices of differentiated complex varietal extra virgin olive oil, this is unlikely. It is likely that highly mechanised groves will produce olive oil efficiently enough to be viable at lower retail prices. It is also likely that discerning customers will continue to pay for branded high quality extra virgin olive oil with its diversity of intensities and flavours.

This brief tour around the world's olive oil producing regions will give the new producer an idea of the competitive trading and cultural environment which they are joining. Continuing professional development with the associated quest for knowledge is pivotal in understanding the olive oil market. The organisational and political activities which control the direction of the global and local industries have a fundamental impact on these markets, creating layers of compliance, market intervention, and a multitude of controls.

Imbalance, Complexity and Disharmony

Producers are the beginning of the supply chain and the lowest level of administration which cocoons the olive oil industry. As the olive oil progresses through many layers to eventually being consumed there are aggregations of interest groups with diverse aims, sometimes in concert, sometimes in competition, often in conflict.

Constant amongst these is the demand that high quality extra virgin olive oil exhibits the positive taste characteristics of balance, complexity, harmony and persistence. These elevated aspirations for the oil are not necessarily upheld by the people in the industry that demands them.

The Battle of the Hemispheres

The first division or layer of complexity are the hemispheres with their seasonal activities six months apart. The growth in southern hemisphere production brings fresh olive oil into the world market six months after the northern hemisphere harvest is complete. The production from the south is relatively small at present and has little impact on overall trading. However, in time, as the volume continues to grow the benefit of having fresh olive oil twice a year may affect purchasing and blending in the main producing and consuming countries.

The production in the hemispheres can be complimentary, and probably will be as the new regions mature. Currently, the competition between the new world, which is trying to break into the market, and the old world, which has up to now controlled the market, has led to some combative campaigns to discredit imports into the new producing countries. These campaigns in Australia, New Zealand, South Africa and the USA have involved testing imported olive oils and publicly releasing the results which allege non-compliance and fraud. While this may, in the short-term, increase the sales of new more expensive locally produced extra virgin olive oils, in the longer term, as the boundaries between local and imported brands become blurred, the campaigns will be seen to have damaged the consumers' perception of olive oil as an ingredient.

The campaigns run by local associations were seen to be biased as the testing initially only included imported brands. In subsequent testing where local brands were included and found to be non-compliant the enthusiasm for this approach to gaining market share diminished. Attempts to mount class actions in the USA based on the testing results failed as the integrity of the testing and replication of the test results to the standard required to withstand the scrutiny of the courts proved problematic.

Importers in some cases responded to these attempts to discredit their brands by testing those of the perpetrators and letting the results be known to the brand owners without going public and causing more damage.

These activities to gain and defend market share are generally carried out by the next representative layer up from the producer. These are the grower associations whose remit is to promote the interest of the growers and provide a unified entity with which governments and other institutions can confer and channel support. The importers and distributors also form associations to represent their interests which often conflict with the producers. An example of this is the attempt instigated by Australia to use two tests additional to those described in the IOC International Trade Standards which are used to control the quality of olive oil traded across borders. The Pyropheophytin (PPP) and Diacylglycerol (DAGS) tests have been used to imply that imported olive oils are degraded in comparison to fresher locally produced oils. Slogans such as 'Fresher is Better' have been used to underpin the effort to persuade consumers to buy local products. This approach seems to ignore the availability of fresher oils coming from the northern hemisphere when local products are six months old and the fact that local products also deteriorate and are not always sold out in a year before the new harvest. The threshold on these tests can be adjusted and used as a non-tariff barrier to imported oils under the guise of presenting higher quality products to consumers. While this may be a laudable ethic and induce consumers to pay higher prices for locally produced oils, it is a tactic to gain market share. Inclusion of these standards in the International Trade Standards has so far been rejected with the campaigns ongoing in Australia and California to have them introduced as national standards in these countries to be applied to all extra virgin olive oils traded.

The assault on the quality of imported extra virgin olive oils has resulted in a lift in the quality of olive oils exported to these countries. This will benefit consumers, but not the local producers who now have to compete with higher quality imports and have lost one of their perceived competitive advantages.

Apart from the public conflict between associations representing importers and local producers undermining the confidence of consumers, the added tests would increase the cost of compliance and eventually increase the cost of extra virgin olive oil. Commercial laboratories, some of which are owned by large producers who advocate additional tests, are set to gain from the returns generated by the burgeoning testing regime. In California, local production meets about 10% of consumer demand in the USA and in Australia around 30% of extra virgin olive oil requirements may be met, in both instances a substantial decrease in imports may leave a vacuum to be filled by competing vegetable oils. The campaigns to include the tests are led, and to some extent funded, by larger producers in both countries which dominate the politics of the associations which rely on their levy funding to operate. In Australia the constitution of the growers' association was changed to entrench the right for the larger producers to nominate three representatives to the board, which appoints the president, and consequently dominate the development of policy and allocation of resources.

It is in the interests of the olive industry at large for everyone who earns a living from olive oil to work together to increase the market share of the product and then compete within the industry for a share of the expanding market. Producer and importer associations need to amalgamate to achieve this and realise that pursuing their separate interests is limiting. There is already a crossover of interests with many of the Australian and Californian producers importing and exporting internationally.

Another possibility with standards being introduced which favour more robust or intense olive oils in export markets is that the consumers will reject the robust flavour and opt for new entrants into the market such as avocado oil or canola oil which have comparative health benefits derived from the fat profile and high smoke points.

Associations

Associations are helpful for producers and importers if their agenda is not hijacked by vested interests and the general welfare of members is no longer the primary aim. Associations can be formed at the local level, regional level, state level and national level. For example in the USA there is the California Olive Oil Council, California Olive Oil Commission, Georgia Olive Growers Association, Texas Association of Olive Oil, Olive Growers of Oregon, Florida Olive Council, Florida Olive Growers Association and the American Olive Oil Producer's Association (AOOPA) representing USA producers and the North American Olive Oil Association (NAOOA), which has some USA producer members, mainly representing importers, some of whom now have packaging facilities in the USA and package locally produced extra virgin olive oil. There is talk of adding another, overarching, layer, an 'Olive Oil Board', to promote research and consumption of olive oil.

It is notable that the senior elected office bearers of AOOPA are senior executives of two of the largest producers in California which have been barred from membership of the Californian Olive Oil Council as their brands include olive oils not produced in the State.

All these 'representative' associations support staff and need membership fees and other sources of funding to support their activities. Representations are made to authorities by many of them on behalf of their members, therefore it is no wonder these authorities may be confused by the requests from this fragmented industry and that their attention and funding is diluted as a result.

Some associations have been formed to differentiate the products of their members through production and quality controls more rigorous than the international trade standards. Examples are the Mastri Oleari based in Milan in Italy and the more recently formed QvExtra! in Spain. Membership of each of these organisations numbers less than 100 and their purpose is to develop a certification which 'brands' the products of members as being of higher quality. These 'quality seal' associations, as well as many grower associations, have a seal which can be included on the label to convince the consumer that the higher price they are paying is money well spent. The back labels of some bottles of extra virgin olive oil may have multiple seals certifying that they are organic under European and importing country standards, they meet the standard of the association and that of the local Denomination of Origin specifications. So many stickers designed to give the consumer confidence. So many service organisations to be supported with fees to administer the certifications all adding to the cost of the product. Then there are the stickers boasting of the awards won in multiple competitions which will be discussed later.

Do all these attempts by associations and local promotional organisations, like PDO Boards, to justify their existence to members and induce them to continue paying membership fees work? Are quality and provenance the most important determinants in a consumer's buying decision? Maybe, and maybe not.

In one of the rare cooperations between the importer and producer associations in the USA a survey was undertaken of existing olive oil users and data published in 2018. Around one quarter of those surveyed identified each of quality, taste and health nutritional value as the primary reason for buying a particular brand. Around 10% cited perceived value and 3% recommendations or reviews. For those who are already committed to buying olive oil, quality is obviously important in the USA. There are many consumers in the USA who do not use olive oil, a survey revealing what would induce them to become users would be more useful in increasing consumption. Perhaps price and perceived value would be a more prominent trigger amongst this group of current non-consumers.

Associations are useful in disseminating information on production and other aspects of preparing the product for the market. Gatherings organised under their auspices provide important opportunities for networking, especially useful for new entrants at both the grower and service provision level. They can also provide a critical mass of clients enabling them to negotiate discounts for members for overheads such as insurance and testing for compliance.

Unfortunately, in many associations, the imperative to acquire income to finance staff and projects, and the reluctance of members to increase membership fees, often means that sponsorships become substantial sources of income. When this occurs the sponsor becomes the client and the importance of the member as the client diminishes. This leads to the objective information disseminated by the association becoming compromised in retaining the sponsorship. For example, nurseries which promote super high-density production are prominent sponsors of association events and conferences worldwide. In serving its members' interests, an association may be well advised to solicit and present independent assessments of the viability of these systems. Will this occur if the sponsorship may be withdrawn?

Many associations rely on unpaid elected office bearers supported by paid staff to provide the administration and public face of the organisation. The benefit to the individuals may be status, commercial advantage gained through access to information, influencing beneficial policy making and other non-financial gains. Some associations have in their constitution that their elected office bearers can participate in projects funded by research grants or other finance solicited by the association. This is a dangerous precedent and can lead to incidents where there is an obvious conflict of interest.

A group of gender-based associations has been established. Looking at the industry elected leadership at international and IOC level women are extremely underrepresented. This is despite there being many high profile female producers and leaders of regional associations. Perhaps in reaction to this, women in Italy established Donne dell'olio and more recently the international 'Women in Olive Oil' (WIOO) NGO has been launched. If these organisations result in more women being elevated to senior elected positions at the IOC it will be a good result and a welcome change from the multitude of group photographs of men in grey suits.

Frustration with existing avenues for representation tends to spawn new dedicated entities to pursue these factional interests. Whether these can be justified or not, the practice is symptomatic of an ailing industry and the fragmentation caused dilutes any effectiveness. The remedy is the provision of leadership which rises above the internecine destruction to deliver a unity of purpose and clear direction with leaders elected on merit and not any other pretext.

Quality Certification

Parallel with producers' associations are the Denomination of Origin Certifications (PDO). Usually overseen by boards of producers and equipped with tasting panels, the purpose is to define the extra virgin olive oils from a given area, monitor the quality and certify compliant products to provide a marketing differentiation.

Some countries require that exports are certified and importing countries may require compliance with local standards. There is a range of certifying associations, some of which are genuinely not-for-profit but pay salaries, some are private enterprise for profit and others are government or institutional agencies. An extra virgin olive oil from a particular PDO in Spain, arriving on the retail shelf in the USA, may have trade standard compliance from International Olive Council accredited tasting panels and chemical testing laboratories, the PDO Certification, QvExtra! quality seal, organic certification, the North American Olive Association Quality Seal and Food and Drug Administration (FDA) certification. Six certifications all based on the same standards, all taking paperwork and time and all requiring quite substantial fees.

An independent analysis of the cost recovery of the testing and certification regime by comparing the sales of the same product, packaged the same way and sold through the same outlets at the same price, with one line having the minimum required compliance certifications and the other having the six and possibly more certifications would make interesting reading.

No wonder extra virgin olive oil ranks as one of the most regulated food products in the world.

The next layer of organisation is the institutional layer, regional and national governments. Regional governments provide research facilities and, in some cases, collect producer levies for this purpose. They lobby national governments on behalf of the producers, packers and distributors and other olive industry services. It is their remit to regulate production and processing facilities regarding environmental and food safety issues. Generally, the laws covering these responsibilities are national with the provinces having some leeway to vary regulations where there are local impacts, for example water usage. Where possible, local laws which can give the province a competitive advantage are introduced, for example the banning of night harvesting in super high-density groves and the promotion of 'bird-friendly' extra virgin olive oils.

Multi-layered Governance

National governments are a higher level of administration and through their departments and research institutions regulate trade, collect taxes, support research and set education and social policy. From country to country the involvement of the levels of government varies; in Greece the advice is 'to work with the government' if one wants to progress an agenda, even if no government funding or support is required. Some enthusiastic young producers who returned to Greece with innovative and fresh ideas to help with the family olive business during the Global Financial Crisis (GFC) privately expressed frustration to me that they could go so far but then were blocked by the bureaucracy. Some were contemplating returning to their pre GFC occupations in other countries. The loss of this core of educated, experienced and internationally connected cohort will not augur well for the Greek olive oil industry. Where there is a substantial bureaucracy controlling an industry, one must question whose interests are served, those of the institutions, the government or the producers?

The research and education system often works very closely with the olive oil industry providing research from production to consumption. Funding for research comes from many sources. Provincial and national governments support research institutions and provide project funding. Institutions also seek funding from private enterprise for more applied research. In some instances, private interests approach universities with funding to undertake research which will support a particular enterprise from which the interests will gain financially.

Politicians, academics, bureaucrats and business people generally have the same aim of increasing their influence and enhancing their importance. Politicians want power to win government and impose their policies, academics want to enhance their profile as researchers or teachers to gain recognition and attract more professional recognition and research funding, bureaucrats are nominally the servants of the politicians and aspire to expanding their influence in government and business people seek the reward of profit for their enterprise to expand its market share.

For success in an industry all those involved need to work in concert to a common aim of increasing the efficiency and productivity of the industry within acceptable social expectations of a reasonable living for all and a justice system which protects everyone. Societies overwhelmed by bureaucracy and centralised control do not foster efficiency and productivity.

Above national governments there are the overarching bureaucracies like the European Union and Free Trade Zones which develop and enact policy across all sectors and member countries. The olive oil industry is but one sub-sector of the agricultural and food sector.

The producer at times must feel very distant and disengaged from all these organisations and institutions and the controls they assert.

In the olive oil industry, there is one international body established and convened to provide leadership and promote a unified approach in the global olive oil industry, the International Olive Council. The following extract is taken from the Council website.:

'

MISSION (WHO WE ARE)

The International Olive Council is the world's only international intergovernmental organisation in the field of olive oil and table olives. It was set up in Madrid, Spain, in 1959, under the auspices of the United Nations. It used to be known as the International Olive Oil Council or IOOC until 2006, when its name was changed.

The Council is a decisive player in contributing to the sustainable and responsible development of olive growing and it serves as a world forum for discussing policymaking issues and tackling present and future challenges. It does so by:

- *Encouraging international technical cooperation on research and development projects, training and the transfer of technology.*
- *Encouraging the expansion of international trade in olive oil and table olives, drawing up and updating product trade standards and improving quality.*
- *Enhancing the environmental impact of olive growing and the olive industry.*

- *Promoting world consumption of olive oil and table olives through innovative campaigns and action plans.*

- *Supplying clear, accurate information and statistics on the world olive and olive oil market.*

- *Enabling government representatives and experts to meet regularly to discuss problems and concerns and to fix priorities for IOC action.*

- *Working in close partnership with the private sector.*

Its current membership includes the leading international producers and exporters of olive oil and table olives. IOC producer Members account for 98% of world olive production, located primarily in the Mediterranean region.

The IOC is committed to the integrated, sustainable development of world olive growing. It attempts to translate this commitment into tangible advancement for its member countries and, most importantly, for the ordinary people who earn their livelihood from the produce of the olive tree.'

Before commenting on my perception of the IOC in achieving its mission from my perspective as a producer, I acknowledge that access to senior executives and managers at the IOC has been available to discuss in person some of these issues. Without endorsing the Savantes taste training programme in any way, the relevant IOC department has supplied samples of defects to be used for training. This has enabled the training to use standard defect samples, when using the samples, the presenters state that their provision is accompanied by a letter from the IOC stating that their provision can in no way be used as an indication of their support. In this way the IOC also supplies samples to other non-endorsed taste training programmes offered by private enterprise.

A mission statement which has multiple objectives makes it difficult to achieve as from time to time there is variable emphasis on objectives, depending on the particular interest of the incumbent leaders. The mission should be singular. Its achievement should enable other secondary objectives to be achieved. Limitations should be acknowledged but not part of the objectives.

Increasing Consumption of Olive Oil

The mission of the IOC should simply be 'To increase the consumption of olive oil and table olives'.

Strategies would then be in order of importance:

- Working in close partnership with the public and private sector.
- Promoting world consumption of olive oil and table olives through innovative campaigns and action plans.
- Updating product trade standards and improving quality.
- Encouraging international technical cooperation on research and development projects, training and the transfer of technology.
- Supplying clear, accurate information and statistics on the world olive and olive oil market.

The major limitation being that all this will be achieved within environmental guidelines. With the increased awareness of environmental issues, it can be argued that if the industry does not adhere to environmental practices which meet the expectation of consumers, consumption of olive products will not increase. A good example of this is the reaction of British consumers and retailers to the publicity given to the killing of migratory birds in Spain during night harvesting of high-density groves.

If the singular aim to increase the global consumption of olive oil is achieved annually the proceeds will generate the funding for research, education and technology transfer. The private sector will profit from trade and have the funds to invest in expansion by supporting promotional campaigns. Governments will be administering a profitable industry through regulation of standards and those covering the social and environmental impact. Political influence of the regions will increase. Data and statistics collected and distributed by the IOC will give accountability that the mission is being achieved and the strategies working.

Meetings and networking amongst government representatives and experts are management tools and should not be part of the mission. The meetings are a means to an end and not an end in themselves.

The IOC claims to represent 98% of world olive oil production. Why then is the organisation expending resources on canvassing membership of the other 2%. The reasons can only be political as justification on financial grounds would seem difficult. These resources would be better spent on establishing relationships with consuming countries and increasing consumption.

As a producer observing from afar, the newsletter and other communications emanating from the IOC report on a plethora of meetings with experts and government representatives and few with the private sector. Successes given publicity seem to be more about increasing membership of the organisation than celebrating increasing consumption.

The overseeing of trade standards is an important strategy facilitating international trade. However, the emphasis on quality through the tasting panel system is tending to define olive oil in technical terms and not as a food and ingredient. It is notable that most of the 80 IOC accredited tasting panels are administered by institutions such as departments of agriculture or universities and the tasters are drawn from their employees and associates with little direct investment in production or consumption. The result is that the technical panels are defining the flavour profiles of olive oil with their own perception of technical perfection with little reference to consumer preference. The trend emerging is a product which is increasing in intensity measured through bitterness and pepperiness which is the preference of tasting panels. This is at a time where in countries such as the USA the bitterness is being bred out of vegetables such as aubergine or eggplant, and irrigated radishes on the grocery shelves are devoid of heat or spiciness.

The IOC does not reference panels comprising consumers which can be used to moderate the activities of accredited technical panels.

The cornerstone of olive oil classification by panels is the IOC Tasting Profile Sheet which in digital form is completed for each oil being evaluated by panellists. The sheet first requires the taster to identify the defects in the oils, having done that they are required to record the intensity of the positive characteristics of fruitiness, bitterness and piquancy or pepperiness.

This process provides the lead for the entire industry tasting cohort, suggesting that detecting defects is the primary reason for tasting with describing the positive flavour profile being secondary. This needs to change with the description of positive flavours being the primary reason for tasting and detection of defects secondary.

The downstream effect of the negative approach to tasting is the over detection of defects which often are positive flavours not experienced by panellists accustomed to assessing oils from a particular region. Anecdotally this is demonstrated in a verbal report by an industry trader who submitted a Tunisian olive oil for assessment to a Spanish panel during the holiday season when less experienced tasters were filling in for their more experienced colleagues who were on holiday. The inexperienced panel deemed the sample defective, when submitted for a second test after the holiday period the sample passed as extra virgin olive oil with no defect. This is a single example of a phenomenon well known in the industry where panels tend to find olive oils from other regions, or different styles, defective when they are not.

A suggestion to the IOC that accredited panels should be sent samples of varieties from different regions to broaden their knowledge was dismissed as too difficult. The problem being that the selection of the samples may imply some bias and attract criticism from countries which felt their varieties were underrepresented. One way of overcoming these complaints would be for the IOC to administer a varietals bank to which countries could submit samples of their varietals for storage and distribute them to panels which wanted to extend their knowledge. Perhaps this would be too hard too, cruelled by the inevitable parochial arguments over collection, storage and distribution protocols.

Quality standards are required to control the integrity of traded products; however, the process and administration of the quality control should not set the flavour profiles on offer. Constant monitoring of consumer preferences is necessary to guide product development with quality control providing the minimum requirements for product integrity.

Advocating change is justified if analysis shows that a particular regime is not working. There is no doubt that the management of the IOC can show that they are achieving many of the objectives in the mission statement – holding meetings, managing standards, consulting with governments, supporting research and education and supporting promotional campaigns.

However, as a producer the most important part of the mission statement comes at the end 'The IOC is committed to the integrated, sustainable development of world olive growing. It attempts to translate this commitment into tangible advancement for its member countries and, most importantly, for the ordinary people who earn their livelihood from the produce of the olive tree.'

The producer rephrasing of this could well be 'The IOC is committed to sustainable profitable olive growing and trading. This will lead to the advancement of those who earn their livelihood from the produce of the olive tree and consequent advancement for its member countries'.

A little perplexed by the use of the description of 'ordinary people' in such a defining document, I looked up the meaning to find the definition: 'with no special or distinctive features, normal'. Setting aside reactive feelings that this is very patronising of the producers and other operatives who are the mainstay of the industry, it does reflect the view of those who are privileged to compile the IOC mission statement that the 'normal' people are some other homogenous and distant beings.

How well is the IOC serving the ordinary people it aspires to advance through expanding a profitable olive oil industry? According to data published in the United States Department of Agriculture Oil Crops Year Book, from 2006 to 2021/22 the consumption of olive oil as a percentage of world vegetable oil has declined from just below 2.5% to just above 1.5%. On the relative growth rate compared with competing vegetable oils olive oil is falling behind fast.

Analysis of the published IOC data on world olive oil production and consumption from 2013/2014 to pre-pandemic year 2019/2020 shows that the annual consumption trend is a flat line along the three million tonnes mark. Data from post 2020 is arguably aberrated by the effects on production and trade by pandemic restrictions, the war in Ukraine and the drought in northern hemisphere countries in 2022.

In six years, there has been virtually no increase in consumption. The production trend starts just below three million tonnes per annum and ends up just above three million tonnes over the same period. The result is that the global industry produced a surplus of around 600,000 tonnes, above the normal year to year carryover stocks of around 300,000 tonnes. As would be expected in a surplus situation the price trendline is down when measured by the import price into the USA, dropping from US$4,500 per tonne in 2013/2014 to US$3,500 per tonne in 2019/2020.

According to their own published data, the IOC has not only presided over a static level of consumption over the last six years, but it has also seen an increase in production which has resulted in a surplus of olive oil globally and a price decline of over 22% per tonne for imports into the USA. Concomitant substantial declines in price occurred in the main producing countries, Spain, Italy and Greece.

It is common practice in organisations when there is a decline in trade in the short-term to be defensive and publicise the long-term trend which tends to demonstrate a more favourable picture. The IOC can boast that from 1990 to 2020 there has been an increase in consumption of olive oil from two million tonnes to three million tonnes per annum, a

50% increase. However, this growth stalled in 2009 and has remained at approximately three million tonnes reached in that year. The 50 percent increase in consumption occurred in 20 years of the 30 quoted with the last 10 showing no increase.

The IOC is not meeting its stated mission to increase the consumption of olive oil. It is meeting its aim of promoting olive growing. By being successful in one aim and not the other a surplus has been created and the prices received lead to the conclusion that its overall commitment to '*advancement for its member countries and, most importantly, for the ordinary people who earn their livelihood from the produce of the olive tree.*' is not being met.

The disturbing observation from this conclusion and consequent search of the industry media and the IOC publications for acceptance of the situation and credible plans is that there don't seem to be any.

On the contrary, a search of the IOC website reveals much activity on regulation, standardisation, diplomacy, research and other esoteric pursuits. There is a dearth of information on consumption and a search using keywords consumption, profit and markets is barren. Where there are tenders invited for promotional activities or reports on activities completed they comprise technical taste training and compliance, targeting institutions.

Questions asked about the responsibility of the IOC for promotion and market expansion have received the answer that these are seen as the responsibility of producing countries. If this is indeed the case and these countries resist efforts by the IOC to lead the industry to increasing consumption and demand and greater prosperity, the system is broken and the decline in competitiveness and profitability will continue.

Looking at the responses of some of the countries to declining consumption in their own domain and importing countries is no more encouraging. In Spain lampante olive oil is being stored to keep it out of the market with the possibility of refining later or use as biofuel. Limiting the supply of commodities to maintain prices does not work. It may work with diamonds where one company has a monopoly, but it will not work with olive oil which can be substituted with another product which with a little modification can mimic all its beneficial properties.

The wool industry in Australia in the 1990s destroyed itself by positioning its product as a fine fibre in the high-end fashion industry and encouraged all producers to get higher prices by producing fine and superfine wool. Very much the same way the olive industry is positioning extra virgin olive oil as a high polyphenol vegetable oil targeting the top end of the market in the hope of attracting high prices. The wool industry collapsed when demand for fine wool declined sharply, and the industry tried to put a floor price in the market by withholding supply and storing the wool. The wool was replaced by artificial fibres which mimicked the properties of fine wool. The same scenario can happen in the olive oil industry if supply is withheld, and the normal dynamics of supply and demand do not set the price.

Another tactic of the Spanish Government is to encourage producers to harvest the olives for olive oil production earlier to produce extra virgin olive oils higher in polyphenols from green olives which give lower yields of oil and potentially higher prices.

This move makes many assumptions which if flawed will only exacerbate the situation. The first is that the so-called higher quality oils will receive a higher price. This will be unlikely if the supply of this category of olive oil increases following the simple equation of supply and demand. Even if higher prices are achieved the need to amortise production costs over a smaller yield may well mean that producers will need the higher prices to retain their profit margins, if prices fall, margins will be severely affected.

Another assumption is that the demand for extra virgin olive oils with higher polyphenol levels and the associated more robust flavour profiles will increase with supply. There does not seem to be evidence that consumers' preference is for more robust flavours, on the contrary what evidence there is points to consumers' preference being for oils with delicate to medium intensities. Add to this the increase in price and the industry will be aiming to produce a product which current consumers may well reject resulting in lower consumption. Persuading consumers who use other flavourless vegetable oils to shift to using medium to robust olive oils at a higher price is unlikely to be successful.

One perceived advantage of more robust olive oils being produced is the increased shelf-life with the deterioration of the oils from oxidation being slower. This will lead to increased carryover stocks between seasons and extend the period of oversupply.

A further assumption of this recommendation of earlier harvesting is that the equipment is available to harvest the Spanish crop over a much shorter period. This is unlikely with the expectation that the harvesting campaign will extend over a period of four or more months in normal seasons. The income for the service suppliers will also be curtailed meaning that the employees will suffer, especially those who rely on income from the campaign as seasonal workers.

Italy has taken a different approach by purchasing olive oil to the value of €20 million for distribution to lower income families. This approach helps maintain the price, works within the current capacity of the industry, reduces the surplus through usage rather than storage, and will be a health benefit to the socio-economic groups which would not normally purchase and use olive oil. An added benefit is that lower-priced competing vegetable oils are deprived of some market share.

There seems to be an obsession in the global olive oil industry administration to encourage higher quality products to increase consumption. This is an industry push, probably by the private sector interests in positions of leadership in industry representative associations who produce at this high-end of the market. They may see it as their remit to promote the higher quality at the expense of the lower priced less robust flavoured olive oil. This selfish approach may enhance their sales, but the profile of olive oil measured by monitoring consumption trends is diminished. There does not seem to be a coordinated international project which has researched and reported on consumer preference with recommendations on how the industry can adjust to accommodate them. The approach seems to be 'this is high quality and good for you, so buy it!' 'Take the high quality road or no road'! Consumption over the last ten years indicates that this approach is not working, and it is time for a rethink.

The Unpalatable Truth

Too often we are critical of our industry's perceived failings without offering some practical solutions. It is the aim of this publication to create an awareness of the various directions, challenges and tensions of the global olive oil industry and to offer to the 'ordinary people' some areas in the wider industry where they can have a positive influence on their well-being.

Reasons for Static Consumption

Here is a list of possible reasons for static consumption, compiled from personal experience, observations and opinions gleaned from conducting conferences and tasting programmes in many producing and consuming countries over the past 25 years. The perspective is also that of a producer and trader of extra virgin olive oil and table olives in Australia.

Consumers and Flavour

- **Consumers generally do not like the flavour of extra virgin olive oil**
  There are too many presumptions about consumer preferences which are not supported by evidence. Surveys often canvass those who already consume olive oil to elicit the triggers for their purchase. Surveys on the potential triggers or inducements needed to attract users of animal fats and other vegetable oils are hard to find. The emphasis seems to be increasing the share of a limited market rather than increasing the market, then competing for an increased share.

  This attitude is evident in the approach of some leaders of the industries in competing countries, Spain, Italy and Greece. An example is the occasion when the leader of a large Italian association openly criticised Spanish production and their style of olive oil product when speaking as a guest at the national Olive Oil Conference in Chicago in the USA. The tone of this criticism was to denigrate Spanish products and increase Italian share of the market. This kind of utterance shows little understanding of consumer reaction and is pure politicking to impress the membership of the association. It is parochial and unedifying.

  Where consumer preferences are canvassed, the survey parameters are skewed, for example those who seek attitudes towards the health benefits of olive oil which preselects a particular socio-economic segment where health is a prime concern.

The surveys are simplistic and do not recognise the segmentation of the existing market of consumers and non-consumers, or the possible preference and potential for all the classifications of olive oil.

The remedy to this shortcoming is for the industry to support independent surveys of consumer preferences for cooking oils and fats in producing and consuming countries on all continents. Some of the leading purveyors of vegetable oils such as Cargill, based in Minneapolis in the USA, annually carry out research on consumer preference across all their products to guide their product development and marketing. The olive industry would benefit from a similar objective approach covering olive oil and competing vegetable oils.

- **There is too much emphasis on quality as perceived by technicians**
  Promotion projects supported by the IOC in regions where olive oil is not produced or consumed in large quantities appear to take the form of formal taste training following the IOC accredited panel method. The targeted audience is mostly institutions, academics and trade compliance.

- **Too much emphasis on robust olive oils**
  The control which the technical tasters in panels and competitions exert over the style of olive oil which is rewarded as high quality and worthy of the gold medals in competitions is too great. The promotion by producers is correlated with the winning of awards which is correlated with the preferences of the judges. At no point is the preference of the non-consumers of olive oil considered, it is a race for market-share of the top five percent of extra virgin olive oils which win awards. The downside of this is that the oils which do not get gold awards are considered lower quality, which they are not, they are still in the top five percent. The difference in scores between the winners and the losers is small and very often affected by subjective judgements and bias.

  The bias and preference of judges in some competitions is well known to some producers who are artful in blending an extra virgin olive oil which will please the palates of the judges in a particular competition. These oils are known as 'show oils' and are not necessarily the oils the consumer will buy if they buy the 'winning' oil off the supermarket shelf.
  Another indication that robust high-polyphenol extra virgin olive oils are more valued by tasting panels and competition organisers, including the IOC, is when

the competition results are announced the results for robust or intense oils are always first, followed by the medium intensity and delicate oils. There is no reason for this other than a subjective judgement by the organisers.

It is correct practice to taste the delicate extra virgin olive oils first so that the palate of the taster is not 'numbed' by the robust oils to the degree that they cannot discern the subtle tastes. It makes sense that the results of the competition should be reported in order of tasting and rising intensity, delicate, medium, robust. The IOC sets the trend with the Mario Solinas Quality Awards media release reporting the results in order of intensity, namely intense green fruitiness, medium green fruitiness, mild green fruitiness then ripe fruitiness.

It would be a very interesting exercise to take the 150 or so extra virgin olive oils entered in the Mario Solinas awards to, for example, the USA and have the oils ranked by a panel of olive oil consumers and a panel of non-consumers. This could be repeated in countries with different cuisines such as China, India and Indonesia to see the preference variation between countries. The results would be a good indication of the gap between the institution-based technicians and the consumers and potential consumers of olive oil.

Unfortunately, an exercise like this is unlikely to find support as it will potentially challenge the beliefs of the decision-makers and require a rethink. On the other hand, it may confirm the direction in which they are going and reinforce their collective wisdom.

In 2020 the first edition of the Milan International Olive Oil Award introduced staged judging. The entries were blind tasted by a panel of professional tasters from the Organizzazione Nazionale Assaggiatori Olio di Oliva (ONAOO) who pre-selected oils to progress to the finals where they were assessed by three juries representing: Horeca food service, journalists and consumers. The award winners and the 'best pick' from each of the juries were published in 2021 in the OlioOfficina magazine (www.olioofficina.it). The ONAOO picked an Italian oil, the journalist jury picked an Italian branded mainstream supermarket oil, the Horeca jury picked a Spanish oil, and the consumer jury picked a Greek oil. In 2022 the number of juries was increased to include an Italian sommeliers' jury, and a large scale and retail chain buyers' jury. All except the buyers selected

different Italian oils as the best, the buyers selected a Spanish oil. On the face of it, it reveals the different preferences in the market segments which should be recognised in an industry sales strategy.
The industry needs more of this sort of progressive action which challenges conventional wisdom. The organisers and juries are to be commended.

- **Consumers are confused by multiple classifications**
Consumers are confused by the multiple classifications of olive oil. They buy olive oil and are then told it is a blend of refined olive oil and extra virgin olive oil and they should be buying extra virgin which is more expensive. They are told that olive pomace oil is not fit for human consumption, but it is on the food store shelves in some countries and used extensively in foodservice.

Extra lite olive oil was on the shelves in some countries and the message was that it is light in colour and flavour, not light in calories. Producers of extra virgin talked up their product as extracted without the use of chemicals and denigrated refined oils as processed using chemicals which were toxic. Some implied that they are solvent extracted like other vegetable oils and the solvents used may be carcinogenic.

In some of the new world producing countries the imported northern hemisphere products were denigrated by stories of the olives being left to fall off the trees before being processed to produce defective oil. While there is a half-truth in this, the full story that this oil was refined to remove defects was not told. This selective publicity perpetrated by those who know such a generalisation is deceitful does immeasurable harm to the consumer's confidence in the olive oil product. Any gains for locally produced products are short-term.

To get a competitive edge some companies introduced 'ultra' or 'super' extra virgin olive oil claiming it is higher quality than 'ordinary' extra virgin because of the lower free fatty acid level. Consumers do not understand free fatty acids which are touted as a measure of the quality of extra virgin olive oil. More confusion.

Health benefits of extra virgin olive oils have become the central message of promotion worldwide, displacing flavour. The health conscious are told the higher the polyphenol level manifested in the intensity of the taste, the healthier the oil is. There is even a competition held every year for 'The World's Healthiest Extra

Virgin Olive Oil' at The Health & Food Extra Virgin Olive Oil Awards Competition in Málaga, Costa Del Sol, Spain. The level of oleocanthal, a polyphenol which has similar anti-inflammatory action to ibuprofen and is responsible for the burning sensation when tasting olive oil, is one of the indicators measured, the higher the level the higher the score. Other measures used are the total polyphenol level and the most balanced fatty acid profile. When asked at a conference in the USA what the healthy 'dose' of oleocanthal required to combat inflammation was, the head of the team from Monell Chemical Senses Center in Washington, which discovered oleocanthal, responded 'we don't know'. This response leads to the conclusion that the claims that the higher the polyphenol level, the healthier the oil are spurious. Our bodies are selective in their absorption and excrete the excess and unwanted nutrients.

An oil with the highest possible polyphenol level which includes the bitter component and the spicy heat is probably too robust for most consumers' palates. To get the health benefit the oil must be consumed. The more robust the oil the less will be used to add flavour while a more delicate oil will require more for the same effect.

Consumers wonder why, given all the publicity about its health benefits - the star or 'traffic light' ratings being introduced in some countries to provide consumers with an independent evaluation of the food products do not give extra virgin olive oil the top rating. The reason is simply that it is almost 100% fat, and the star ratings tend to discourage the excess consumption of fats without differentiating between 'good' and 'bad' fats.

Currently, in some countries such as Italy and the USA, producers and distributors are calling for yet another classification for extra virgin olive oil for those which meet more stringent quality specifications. This is sure to confuse consumers even more and is a reaction to the failure to sell the benefits of the existing classifications.

Competing seed oils such as canola, sunflower and soybean are being engineered to produce high oleic vegetable oils equalling the monounsaturated fat profile of olive oil and neutralising this health claim as a marketing edge. Avocado oil has a very similar fatty acid profile to olive oil.

Consumers need to receive a clear and simple message which gives them a good reason to buy olive oil, in particular extra virgin olive oil, over animal fats and other vegetable oils. Extra virgin olive oil has a unique combination of sustainability, purity, tasty, and healthy distinctions which can be measured and justify the higher price in terms of value for money.

Producers and traders need to learn that campaigns which denigrate classifications of olive oil other than the ones they are selling damages the overall category and indirectly affect consumption and eventually their own bottom line.

- **There does not appear to be a tier of less technical training and promotion to consumers.**
  The emphasis by the IOC on standardisation covers the tasting method for classification of olive oils by panels. Considering the impact of the evaluation by panels on the price received for the product, consistency in this process across all jurisdictions is important. However, the formal technical process for classification is not appropriate for less formal promotions to consumers.

  The pre-eminence of the technical panel members has created a tasting elite and the consequent reluctance to share this status. This elite is used by the IOC for its Mario Solinas competition and by many other competitions for their juries. Examination of the employment and industry involvement of these panellists shows they mainly come from government, academia, research or technical service industries. There are few consumers or producers on the panels resulting in a skewing of training towards the promotion of more robust extra virgin olive oils which are the style preference of the so-called elite tasters, rather than the more delicate and medium intensity olive oils which are preferred by mainstream consumers.

  The remedy for this is to encourage a rigorous less formal tasting method for consumers. Existing tasting programmes organised and presented by private enterprise which meet stated criteria for integrity could be accredited by the IOC. Individuals who pass prescribed taste tests could be certified as 'taste advocates' and promotion campaigns encouraged to use them instead of, or in addition to, panel tasters. This will increase the number of promotional activities, make them more related to different consumer environments and include more private enterprise which is responsive to consumer demand.

Research into consumer preference could be fed to the 'taste advocates' to keep them abreast of trends in the country in which they are operating.

- **Promotion often requires consumers to taste the raw oil**
  Tasting oil is an acquired practice, other than those involved in the assessment of oil for trade or cooking, it is the exception to find a consumer who readily tastes olive oil. Yet, at food shows, farmers' markets, trade shows and in many other situations where olive oil is offered for tasting, it is offered raw.

  Olive oil is a food ingredient and should be offered to consumers for tasting in food. It is not complicated to do this, a mayonnaise or aioli made with olive oils from different varietals demonstrates the difference in flavour effect. The same can be done with tomato soup, homemade or bought in a supermarket. Cut-up vegetables can be provided to dip into the oil rather than bread. The suggestion that the oil should be used in food must be ever present.

  Visitors to the Summer Fancy Food Show in New York will observe that the aisles where free food tasting is offered are packed, whereas the aisles offering olive oil for tasting in cups or with bread from Tunisia, Turkey, Greece, Spain and Italy are virtually empty, populated mainly by through traffic.

  The olive oil industry needs to use every culinary trick available to induce more people to taste and use our product. The industry aspires to change the mindset of consumers, perhaps it is the industry which needs to change its mindset and see the product from the potential consumers' perspective.

  One trick is to use 'olive oil powder' which is made by mixing extra virgin olive oil with tapioca maltodextrin. This results in a powder which smells like the olive oil used and when tasted gives the taste of the olive oil. Care should be exercised in selecting a maltodextrin with the lowest level of sweetness. While not perfect, the method gets past the revulsion of tasting olive and as the maltodextrin melts in the mouth the flavours of the extra virgin olive oil are quite apparent. The mixture keeps for a while in the fridge so can be prepared in advance. The powder is a talking point and can be presented on the side of a plate to be used, for example, for sprinkling on a Caprese salad to add the extra virgin olive oil.

An excellent example of how to taste the flavours of different varietal olive oils in food was presented at a QvExtra! conference in Cordoba, Spain. Prepared by chef Alberto Moya with the assistance of a local culinary school, lunch guests were presented with three Spanish varietals (arbequina, picual and hojiblanca) in different dishes. First the extra virgin olive oil was tasted, then the table olive from that variety, then in order, salmarejo, Russian salad, mussels and finally a small cake or doughnut. Each sample was prepared with the same ingredients with only the extra virgin olive oil used being different. The whole experience was a brilliant concept and edifying. The different impact of the olive oils on the flavour of the samples was quite clear and the discussion at the end of the tasting was animated. One nuance detected by some tasters was that all the samples with the hojiblanca extra virgin olive oil tasted saltier than the other samples. When asked why, the chef revealed that when using this varietal he always needed less salt as in some way it accentuated the salty taste of a dish. Perhaps a selling point if the perception can be supported by science and using hojiblanca reduces the intake of salt for those suffering from hypertension.

The lunch was logistically challenging with over 220 guests needing almost 4000 samples at some considerable cost. However, it was memorable, and the impact was well worth the investment as it has been copied to an equal or lesser degree many times since.

- **Consumers are educated**

  Those who use vegetable oil or animal fats need to be persuaded to use olive oil, and users of olive oil encouraged to use extra virgin olive oil. The universal panacea offered by producers and others along the chain to retailers is to 'educate' the consumer. This attitude is unproductive suggesting that the purveyor of olive oil has the knowledge which must be taught to the 'ordinary' people. The approach could be described as 'superior' or 'elitist', a view supported by the choice of venues for some olive oil industry events such as university campuses and exclusive restaurants or city clubs.

  The term 'consumer' is used to cover the diversity that is the population which purchases food. This can be segmented into many socio-economic groups separated by purchasing power, ethnicity, locality and many other criteria. Everyone is educated to some degree, especially in the demands of daily life and the acquisition of food. For some who live a subsistence life, seeking food is the sole activity for the day, for others it is covered by a once weekly visit to the food store or grocery to buy the week's supply. Between these two extremes there is every level of preference and disposable income which must be allocated to food and other essential or luxury items. An interesting and pertinent attempt to measure the affluence of society is the Living Standards Measure or LSM used in populations which have a high Gini index, or Gini ratio, which is a measure of the income or wealth inequality of a group of people. The measure allocates a score to a basket of possessions and services for a particular household as a measure of their purchasing power.

This approach would provide useful data for the preparation of a marketing plan for olive oil, backed up by data providing information on consumers' purchasing decisions when it comes to cooking fats. It can be postulated that there will be many different segments, each of which will require a different approach. Some decisions will be price-based, others on location and/or ethnicity, some religious. It may be that for those in the lower deciles of the LSM the sale of cheaper refined olive oil blends with other vegetable oils will be the entry point. As the populations move up the LSM scale a combination of blends, refined olive oil and extra virgin olive oil will be offered. Each market will be targeted with a specific message which meets the aspirations of that group, in some cases flavour, others health and overall improvement and prosperity of their life.

Then there is the promotion and marketing to the users of olive oil which should be aimed at improving the quality of the olive oil they use, lifting them from use of refined olive oils to extra virgin olive oil and increasing the volume used in households.

Consumers are not an uneducated mass waiting for enlightenment on the benefits of olive oil from a self-proclaimed elite who assume their knowledge is superior. The promoters of olive oil need to recognise that it is effective communication and not education which will increase the consumption of all classes of olive oil. Effective communication involves engagement between the recipient and sender on common ground which creates awareness, establishes a relationship of trust and then leads to a transaction of mutual benefit. Very different from the current 'educate' the consumer attitude of many in the olive oil industry. The lack of success of this approach is reflected in the IOC data which shows no increase in global consumption in the last ten years

- **There are few competitions where oils are judged by consumers**
  The Covid-19 pandemic affected the olive oil industry in many ways. The supply chain was disrupted, and costly safety measures were introduced from harvesting to retail. The hotel and restaurant sectors of the Horeca channel were shut down with immediate impact on the use of olive oil in foodservice. People were forced to stay at home in isolation and home cooking once again became the norm. Retail sales of olive oil increased and online sales became more popular. The overall sales of olive oil fluctuated as people hoarded prior to lockdown then used up the supplies before returning to a more normal purchasing pattern. The impact of redundancies started to have an effect as the decline in disposable income forced consumers to purchase cheaper cooking oils. At the time of writing the aftermath of the pandemic is still disrupting many aspects of the industry and it is expected to take some time to stabilise and reach a new equilibrium. The overall result will probably be a decline in consumption worldwide making better and coordinated promotion an imperative.

  Travel and gathering in groups were banned in most countries disrupting training programmes, trade fairs, conferences and associated extra virgin olive oil competitions. Innovative ways to 'establish' virtual trade fairs were developed and to some degree continued to give traders the opportunity to promote their products.

  Competitions were severely affected. Some were fortunate to complete the judging process prior to the lockdowns, others were caught between receiving the samples and the judging process, these competitions were either cancelled or proceeded with 'remote' judging processes. The degree of rigour in the judging declined as the process became more dispersed and the relevance of the awards was widely questioned on social media. The decisions by organisers to proceed with unconventional remote judging rather than cancelling and reimbursing those who had entered raised the question whether profit has been put before integrity.

  The number of competitions for extra virgin olive oil has burgeoned with many annual competitions in growing and consuming regions, often divided into the northern hemisphere and southern hemisphere. However, there are very few judged by consumers. The rigour of the entry requirements varies considerably and is mainly predicated on the commerciality of the competition, the more commercial the lower the entry requirements so as not to limit the number of entries. The expertise of the judging panels or juries also varies from accredited panels, current or former panel members to those who have attended courses of varying length. For the latter there is no competency test prior to participating in a jury.

Some competitions engage an international jury, others use local tasters. The cost of travel, accommodation and fees for the jurists plays a large part in the experience and composition of the panel. There is considerable prestige in being a jurist and many do not ask for a fee considering the acquired status to be adequate recompense. A study of the jury members for competitions across the world reveals a small group judge in multiple competitions, as many as four. In general, there seems to be considerable turnover of judges which brings a range of experience and preference to competitions. One of the benefits of Covid-19 pandemic was to compel some national competitions to engage an entirely new group of judges from their region and break the nexus between competition organisers and the mutual inclusion arrangements which appear to exist in some cases.

There are at least two competing sites which aggregate the competition results into the world's best olive oil ranking. One, the 'World's Best Olive Oils' has rigorous criteria to allocate competitions into two tiers, the top tier comprises three competitions, the second tier comprises four more. The scores are allocated according to the awards won in each tier and aggregated to declare the 'world's best extra virgin olive oil' each year. At the time of writing the president of the organisation is on the jury of one of the competitions in the top tier which may be perceived as a conflict of interest.

It is to the advantage of the competitions to be included in this ranking as producers who seek the accolade of the world's best olive oil will ensure that they enter all seven competitions. Given that four of the competitions are based in Spain and Portugal and two in Italy with associated loading of regional judges, the ranking can be expected to favour Spanish, Italian and Portuguese extra virgin olive oils. The other competition is based in Canada. The ranking also favours the producers who can afford to enter multiple competitions and have a stipulated quantity of the extra virgin olive oil which they enter.

The other aggregation is the 'EVOO World Ranking' which ranks the winners of 30 competitions worldwide.

Before going into the merits of the many competitions, it must be said that, in general, extra virgin olive oil competitions are good for the industry when they are held to compare the quality of entries, encourage improvement and reward high quality. They are not so good when the organisation is slipshod and does not adhere to processes which give all entries an equal chance, or the organisers make substantial commercial gain which becomes the driving force.

The basic criteria which would be expected in a competition should be:

- Entries must be accompanied by a current certificate of compliance with international trade standards for chemical and sensory specifications from an IOC accredited panel to assure they are extra virgin olive oil.
- Storage of the oils should abide by best practice guidelines.
- The judges or jury should have a certified level of expertise and/or undergo a pre-judging competency test to assure currency.
- No judges or organisers should have an interest in any of the entries and judges must not be privy to the list of entries.
- The tasting and judging of the oils should be 'blind' in that the brand or origin should not be evident in any way.
- Any medal stickers or publicity used by the winners or awardees should only apply to the oil that won the award and should not be used on any other container.
- Samples of all the oils entered should be kept for a period after the judging in case there is a dispute.
- The judging process should be transparent and preclude any particular judge or judges having undue influence.

This is a stringent set of criteria and only a few competitions cover them all.

Starting at the local level, each locality, PDO and region probably has a quality competition and will generally use local judges. These competitions serve the purpose of assuring the quality emanating from the region, that they adhere to a prescribed chemical and flavour profile, comparing the product from different producers and gauging the characteristics of the season's extra virgin olive oils. The information gained is useful for producers and the local administration to ascertain data for planning of training and marketing. At this level the judges are usually from the region and a familiar style expected. They may well have an indirect interest in a product through providing services. One of the limitations of these local competitions is that they promote conformity with local styles, thereby discouraging the quest for new and different flavour profiles.

There are national competitions in producing countries held by government departments such as the annual Spanish Ministry of Agriculture, Fisheries and Food 'Food Award from Spain Best Extra Virgin Olive Oils'. The quality compliance for these awards is stringent and the juries technically highly competent.

Some national competitions are organised by associations which limit entries to the products from members of the country where the competition is held. For example, New Zealand stages a national competition for their country's production and uses mainly local judges to form the jury. The requirements for certification of the entries varies, none of these competitions require the full certification of the extra virgin olive to international trade standard. This is common amongst national and international awards where the chemical and flavour testing usually requires the proof of a limited range of tests which the organisers consider give them reasonable confidence in the integrity of the oil. The cost of a full testing regime for each entry would severely limit the number of entries, especially from small producers. Not requiring the full range of tests does open the possibility of awarding a medal or best on show to an extra virgin olive oil which does not meet international trade specifications, especially on the chemical profile.

Some associations, 'not for profit' organisations and some commercial interests organise national and international competitions. Most of these do need some minimal compliance testing prior to accepting an entry. Others, including some that claim to be the most prestigious, do not require certification other than for organic oils, however they do reserve the right to have entries chemically tested. The number of entries tested is not revealed, one must assume that the cost of testing would limit the number checked. As stated earlier the requirement for full international trade standard sensory and chemical testing would greatly increase the cost of entry and most likely substantially reduce the number of entries. In some cases, indemnities agreed to by the entrants relieve the organisers of any responsibility for the quality, compliance or integrity of the product.

The most rigorous award is the Mario Solinas Quality Award administered by the International Olive Council. It is also seen as the most prestigious amongst the main growing regions in Europe. The conditions of entry require the taking of samples from a tank of a prescribed volume and overseen by a notary public. The tank is then sealed. The samples are sent to the IOC and fully tested for classification as extra virgin olive oil. Official accredited panels then assess and score the oils and the winners are declared. The tanks of the winners are then unsealed and the oil packed with each bottle bearing a numbered label assuring the buyer that the olive oil is the same as the award-winning oil. The rigorous entry requirements and the volume of oil stipulated for entry limits the number of entries compared to the less rigorous more commercial competitions.

Attempts by the IOC to organise a Southern Hemisphere Mario Solinas Quality Award Competition to allow for the different harvesting seasons between the hemispheres have not been successful. To spread the influence of the rigorous process the organisation also introduced a scheme to officially accredit other competitions which complied with a series of criteria similar to those of the Mario Solinas Quality Award. This initiative also seems to have faltered, no doubt because the stringent rules and lack of subsidies for entry fees making the competitions attract few entries and be financially unviable. Entries in the Mario Solinas usually number around 130 compared to some other commercial international competitions which claim to have between 500 and 1,000 entries.

The competition attached to the annual Ovibeja agricultural fair in Portugal is almost as rigorous requiring full compliance certification of entries prior to submission and chemical testing of the award-winning extra virgin olive oils. The rules covering the packaging and distribution of the winning oils are less stringent than Mario Solinas.

From the Mario Solinas and Ovibeja awards the rigour of the testing, tasting and trading of the winning oils declines. Producers should be aware of the aims, entry cost and indemnities associated with each competition before entering. Studying the juries, the experience and regional origins of the judges, the purpose of the organisers and the location of the competition should give the producer good indications of which to enter. Local and national competitions give a good idea of the comparative qualities of the product. International competitions are often entered to strategically position a product in a foreign market, for example entering competitions in the USA as a precursor to entering the USA market.

Additional to the competitions held exclusively for olive oil are those where an olive oil category is part of wider food awards. Examples are the sofi™ awards presented by the Specialty Food Association in the USA and 'The Great British Food Awards' in the United Kingdom. Winning awards in these places the olive oil product in a food context and is useful in promoting directly into the food industry. Judges in these events are usually less technical in their assessment of the olive oil and more consumer oriented.

The food competitions are the closest olive oil gets to having an assessment by consumers. There is no internationally well-known olive oil competition where the jury consists entirely of lay-people, knowledgeable users of olive oil who are not trained to taste according to the technical tasting procedure. As stated earlier it would be an interesting exercise to take the Mario Solinas Quality Award winners and have the oils tasted and ranked by a consumer panel in various countries.

The launch in 2020 by online Italian industry magazine OlioOfficina of the 'Milan International Olive Oil Competition', with judging by technical and consumer juries breaks the mould of competitions judged entirely by technical tasters.

There are many reasons for entering one's olive oil products in competitions, mainly to have a comparative assessment with competing oils and to gain a commercial advantage from publicity by displaying the award label on the product. With the multitude of competitions available and the large number of awards presented the currency of gold medals is being devalued. In the trade there are some competitions deemed more prestigious than others and will probably give a better return on investment in the entry fees and delivery costs. Be wary of the spurious claims by publicity from the organisers that their competition is the most prestigious and the extra virgin olive oils that win awards are the world's best olive oils. The claims are unsubstantiated and no more than marketing spin.

The development of remote tasting for judging of competitions with the restrictions associated with the pandemic is a response to an extraordinary situation. The process, which in some cases has not been transparent, has been called into question by some producers. The double-handling of samples, transferring the contents to small containers, shipping to the location of the jurists with associated risk of poor storage and handling may influence the profile of the extra virgin olive oil. The rigour of the tasting cannot be controlled as it is when all judging is at one location. The reduced expense of staging the judging through savings on jury travel, accommodation, fees and venue hire may make this remote judging attractive to organisers of future events. The lack of rigour should make producers seriously consider not entering these events as the results may well be discredited in the marketplace.

Entering extra virgin olive oils in competitions is a useful quality control and marketing tool. Producers should be selective about the events entered based on return on investment, the market being targeted and the reputation of the competition and competency of the judges. Reading the fine print on the entry form is important to understand the indemnities the organisers demand, some going as far as requiring those entering their products to legally defend the organisers in some circumstances. Be aware of the commitments made by signing an entry form. Winners may also be required to purchase the awards, another way in which some commercial competitions make money.

There is little if any independent analysis which provides comparative data on the return on investment in entering competitions. Most of the quotations from winners about the value of their achievement are anecdotal and not backed by data on improved sales.

Another practice which is deceptive is filling bottles with oils other than the winning extra virgin olive oils and affixing the gold medal sticker or decal on the bottle. There is no policing of this practice and no record of a prosecution or other legal action being taken against a producer or competition for misrepresenting the contents of the bottle. Given the lack of sample retention by competition organisers, any case would be difficult to prove. The application of an award decal for one year's harvest is sometimes applied to a subsequent year's production. The consumer should check that any awards claimed on the bottle pertain to the year of production of the olive oil they are about to buy.

- **Positive flavours should be given precedence over negatives**
  As has been said before, there is too much emphasis on fault/defect detection. The formal process for tasting olive oil advocated and overseen by the IOC encourages

the detection of flavour defects before looking for the positive flavour characteristics of olive oil. Extending this process beyond the panels charged with classifying olive oil is training an entire industry to think defects first and positive attributes second.

The remedy is to change the process promoted by the IOC to dictate that positive attributes are described first with defects second. Unfamiliarity amongst accredited panels of flavours from varietal oils from different regions can be overcome by distributing samples from these varietals to panels for taste training. Events which expose tasters to a multitude of regional varieties should be encouraged.

- **Funding is used to advance agendas**

  The expectation is that funding for promotion to consumers comes from institutions.

  'He or she who pays the piper calls the tune'. Institutions control the flow of money for projects and use the allocation to advance their own agendas. Consequently, the levies and taxes collected at all levels of the olive industry by governments are redistributed to support projects which are not necessarily in the best interest of producers and increased consumption and prices. Administrations have advisory boards which are charged with representing the interests of the levy payers. Often these appointments are political and lip service is paid to the consultation process and accountability is lacking.

  Action to be taken to improve this process is to bring the accountability for promotion closer to the producers by having projects and promotions under closer direction by their associations.

  Encouragement should also be given for small groups to promote their own products to consumers by offering events for which the consumer pays. This will ensure that the events recognise and understand the purchase preferences of consumers. The current expectation is that there is a funding flow which will pay for these to be provided to consumers for free, resulting in the objectives of the promotions meeting the agenda of the funding providers. More effective promotions are those instigated by producers who can sell their products or services directly to consumers. This brings the user and producers close together and the messages do not get confused by layers of vested interests which amend the communication to suit their own ends.

A local, regional, national and international online register of these events would improve attendance. Unfortunately, the resulting devolvement of promotion may draw consumers attention away from the mega campaigns organised by other interests which will be manifest in a reluctance to establish and maintain the international register.

- **More emphasis needed on consumer conversion, loyalty and advocacy**
  National and international promotional campaigns sponsored by governments and undertaken by industry organisations or marketing companies have grand generic titles such as 'Believe in Olive Oil' or 'Great Olive Oil' and 'Olive Oil World Tour'. Millions of euros and dollars are spent on promoting olive oil from the regions funding the promotion with little publicised accountability on how much the campaign has improved the consumption of olive oil.

  Experience shows that marketing companies are loath to be tied to proving that their campaign has led to an increase in sales of a product, success tends to be measured in terms of 'awareness' through glossy brochures or books distributed, the number of media articles detected by media monitors and the number of likes or 'clicks' on social media.

  Clearing out some dusty books I came across a 2011 publication sponsored by the European Union and Spain entitled *'The surprisingly, marvellous, savoury, curious, healthy, historic, artistic and fantastic world of Olive Oil'*. It is a beautiful informative book. The first significant pictorial of food comes on the 27th page. The preceding pages are full of production data, varietals, mythology, olive oil classifications and pictures of the olive groves of Spain stretching to the horizon.

  The question is does it sell olive oil to the consumer or is it a little self-indulgent, trying to satisfy those who paid for it first, the publisher, the producer organisations, the politicians and secondly persuade, incidentally, consumers? Is it trying to portray each of the facets described in the title? It will have made money for the graphic artists, the designers, the authors and the administrators, but what is the return to producers? In the last 10 years since the publication of this book, it seems our industry narrative and method have not changed, and global consumption has not increased.

If the increase in consumption in many of the countries targeted is the measure of success of the collective promotions, the money has been poorly spent. 'Ah' the promoters will say, imagine what will have happened if there had been no promotion at all, consumption may have declined. Well, it has in some countries such as Greece and Spain who have undertaken promotions of their products abroad. If in countries which are the largest users of olive oil consumption is declining and the publicity cannot reverse the trend, what hope is there of convincing other countries to consume copious amounts of olive oil to compensate for the loss of sales in the producing regions?

Research on the awareness and consideration of olive oil amongst consumers in different countries will give data for the mandarins to decide where to invest their promotion dollars. My perception is that there will be enough awareness and consideration stimulated by prior campaigns to justify a shift to targeting the aware and convert them to the use of olive oil of all qualities. At the same time, attention should be given to the converted to assure their loyalty and encourage them to become advocates. In the post-covid world where international travel and gathering in groups will be curtailed for a while, the responsibility for promotion needs to be decentralised. This is good marketing in any environment but necessitates the relinquishing of some control and entrusting a cohort who are local, professional, knowledgeable and innovative. Not only will this expand the pool of advocates, but it also gives the opportunity for them to earn an income from their activities which is correlated with their appeal and efficiency rather than their ability to lobby and write project proposals in search of third-party funding. It will also feed back innovative ways of converting consumers which can be added to the list of approved methods. The creativity of a wide range of advocates in many countries will be encouraged.

Pricing

- **The price is too high**
  Olive oil, and extra virgin olive oil in particular, is more expensive than other vegetable oils and animal fats. Much of the challenge in promoting extra virgin

olive oil is convincing consumers that the benefits of flavour and health justify the higher price.

There seems to be little independent research on the impact price has in a consumer's decision not to buy olive oil. Most of the research is directed at the importance of price for those who already use olive oil, the cohort being surveyed has already made the commitment to pay more. Anecdotally price is quoted most frequently as the reason why consumers don't use olive oil, or if they do they use it sparingly for 'finishing' or on special occasions.

To overcome this resistance to price consumers must be convinced that olive oil, refined, blended or extra virgin, is the best value for money. This will require developing a rating system similar to the star or traffic light system used by the food industry. Developing the rating system will most likely be opposed by those whose products do not rate well, however, consumption of the whole category will lift along with that of their product.

The rating system should include smoke point, intensity, flavour, and fatty acid profile. A possible system will be discussed later.

- **Trade barriers limit supply**
  The dynamics of the politics and trade agreements is yet another layer with which the olive oil producer has to contend. Often unrelated to the olive industry, decisions are made for ideological reasons or self-interest over which the individual industry participant has no control and little, if any, say. An example is the 25% tariff placed on the imports of Spanish packaged olive oil in response to the EU subsidies of Airbus which it is claimed disadvantaged Boeing.

  Subsidies are a tool to give an advantage to a particular industry to correct perceived disadvantages caused by a skewing of investment or socio-economic circumstance. In the olive industry subsidies are provided by almost every government in every growing region. The amount may be predicated on the number of trees or olive oil production, paradoxically subsidies are sometimes paid for producers not to produce at all. Some of the payments are visible and readily identified as subsidies, others are veiled as investment grants, capital incentives, water rights, export concessions, tax relief and so on. All are subsidies delivered in a multitude of ways.

Tariffs on imports may be used as a punitive measure or to limit the competitiveness of imports when a country is developing an industry, or an established industry is threatened by cheap imports. Tariffs and subsidies can be used in concert with local production being subsidised and imports taxed.

Countervailing duties are form of punitive tariff applied where it is established that another country is 'dumping' a product in an importing country at a price which is below the cost of production. This may be for political and fiscal reasons to remove surpluses in the country of origin or as a long-term strategic move to destroy an industry in the destination country with a view to supplying the depleted market.

Non-tariff barriers are used to circumvent World Trade Organisation rules on trade or trade agreements. They may be higher quality standards, environmental or a host of other selective sanctions which may or may not give a financial advantage. An example is the attempt by the Australian and United States olive oil industries to introduce the PPP and DAGs tests as additional standards to the International Trade Standard. The ability to adjust the specifications for compliance with these tests will allow the level to be set to favour locally produced fresher oils over imports. The campaign is run under the guise of assuring better quality products for consumers in those countries.

Two tests which are becoming a requirement for exports to some countries are the MOSH and MOAH tests. Mineral Oil Saturated Hydrocarbons (MOSH) and Mineral Oil Aromatic Hydrocarbons (MOAH) are food contaminants which may be harmful to humans. They are probably derived from printing inks used in food packaging material which migrate into the food. They may also come from lubricating agents in harvesting and processing machinery which are becoming more prevalent with the increased mechanisation of olive oil production.

Biosecurity issues may cause a country or region to ban or limit the movement of machinery, products or plant material. The prevention of the spread of Xylella fastidiosa, a disease which kills olive trees, is an example where areas have been quarantined, buffer zones created with the removal of trees and the movement of olive products restricted. Usually restricted to plant material and not olive oil, the biosecurity regulations will apply to containers, equipment and other consumables coming from the quarantined region. Travellers will also be urged to be mindful of the possibility of spreading diseases on shoes, sporting equipment, clothing and souvenirs.

Trade agreements between countries are a mechanism for by-passing many of the tariffs and establishing mutually beneficial trade in certain commodities and services. However, an agreement between countries or a trading block can be a disadvantage to countries not included.

The list of reasons why global consumption of olive oil is not increasing is extensive and the actions needed to overcome the perceived problems are politically fraught and difficult. There needs to be a fundamental shift in the thinking of all those involved in production, distribution and consumption from focussing on the product to focussing on the people who use it.

The Mediterranean Diet is Only One of Many

- **Promotion concentrates on the role of olive oil in the Mediterranean diet**
  It is understandable that the Mediterranean origins of olive oil and the associated food put the Mediterranean lifestyle at the forefront of the promotion by the main producing countries, Spain, Italy and Greece. However, promoting a diet and associated lifestyle is far harder than promoting a single ingredient. Success in adopting a diet requires a complete change in the production, buying and cooking habits of entire nations which for centuries have consumed a different diet.

  The collective name 'Mediterranean diet' incorporates the food of the many countries around the Mediterranean. The cuisines of Spain, Italy, Greece, France, the Middle East and North Africa are quite different – so which diet is being promoted? It is the nutritionally balanced ingredients of this collection of foods which merits promotion, not the country or region of origin. The countries are also coastal which means they have access to fresh fish, a staple of their diets which not all countries have.

  The supply chain must deliver all the ingredients of the new diet at affordable prices and be accessible. Perhaps this is the attraction to the promoting countries because the promotion covers many products from the region and the funding is seen to enhance consumption of a broad range of consumables.

An example of the Mediterranean lifestyle being central to millions of Euros of promotion is the recent 'Olive Oil World Tour' campaign delivered by the Spanish Olive Oil Interprofessional with support of the European Union. The website describes it as 'An invitation focused on travellers from all over the world to join the European healthy lifestyle through the consumption of olive oil.' The slogan is 'Join the healthy European lifestyle. Let's make a tastier world'.

Here again there are multiple aims, join the European lifestyle, consume olive oil and make a tastier world. The pictures on the campaign website are of lounges setup at airports and other travel hubs intended to attract travellers in transit and expose them to raw olive oil tastings with very little food in sight. Has it fallen into the trap of training people to taste olive oil rather than encouraging them to use it in food, when cooking classes or comparative tastings in food may be more persuasive? What is the measure of success of this expensive campaign – travellers through the door, brochures handed out, contact details collected? It should be the degree to which the promotion has directly increased the consumption of olive oil, a figure hard to establish, given all the other factors which can affect olive oil consumption and trade in a country. These promotions continue to create awareness and may be some 'consideration', but where is the proof of 'conversion'?

A study of Google trends in the USA presented at the Olive Oil Conference in the USA in 2019 shows that the promotion of the Mediterranean diet has had some impact on the searches using this subject line. A search on olive oil over the same period shows a flat trendline. If the promotion of the Mediterranean diet was increasing the chance of conversion to olive oil, one would expect the searches on olive oil to follow the upward trend of the diet.

As a producer of olive oil in the new world outside the Mediterranean countries it makes no sense to tie the promotion of our product to a diet which is foreign to so many ethnic groups. In multicultural countries like Australia and the USA populated by immigration, there are many styles of cuisine in people's homes and on offer at restaurants and other food outlets. It makes sense to tailor our marketing pitch to the different cuisines and promote the attributes of olive oil which enhance them.

Research shows that different ethnic groups have different taste preferences attributable to their genetic make-up as well as the acquired taste from the dominant cuisine. Designing olive oil blends to suit these flavour preferences and couching the promotion in the language of the traditional or staple food should attract more attention leading to sales. Instead of describing the flavours of olive oil in terms of Mediterranean ingredients when selling to the Chinese market, the flavours should be described in terms of the ingredients used in Chinese cooking.

Much research funding allocated to universities in Europe is directed to research on the health benefits of the Mediterranean diet. This induces research institutions in other countries to pursue funding to expand their ambit by indirectly promoting the diet. The olive industry would be better served if more of this funding from the EU and its member countries was directed at researching the health benefit of olive oil in other diets – Asian (China, India, Japan, Indonesia and others), Eastern European, North American, South American, and African. Once the consumption of olive oil has increased in the diets of these countries it may open the door for promotion of other ingredients of the Mediterranean diet.

My personal observation of the narrow focus of promotion of the use of olive oil across ethnicities and social divisions relates to South Africa and the USA. In the former country where over 90% of the population is black or coloured, the olive industry is almost entirely owned and managed by the white population. This is reflected in the official olive oil tasting panel managed by the growers' association being comprised almost entirely of 'white' palates. Consequently, there is little recognition of the traditional food of the black people and promotion of olive oil to this market is almost non-existent. In the USA the Afro-American population is around 12%, the same proportion as those of Hispanic origin, between them they total 25% of American consumers. However, the attendance of these groups at the annual Olive Oil Conference over a period of five years appears to be close to zero, and little attempt was made to attract their attention through presenters representing their food or market potential. This is despite some research into the ethnicity of olive oil consumers indicating that Afro-Americans in the north-eastern States were amongst the highest consumers.

Some of the decline in the consumption of olive oil in Mediterranean countries is probably attributable to the reported decline in adherence to the diet, especially among young people and children. The World Health Organisation (WHO) in 2018 reported that taking in data from 21 European countries indicates that in Greece, Italy and Spain more than four per cent of primary school age children are severely obese. One of the reasons offered is the influx of high calorific convenience foods from countries outside the Mediterranean shifting consumption away from the traditional diet. Ironically, while the Europeans are trying to convince the North Americans to adopt their diet, they are losing ground to the American fast-food diet in their own countries. It should be easier to reverse the decline in adherence to the diet at home than try to persuade other countries to adopt it. No matter how much money is poured into promotional campaigns it is highly unlikely that the population of the USA, India and China will adopt the Mediterranean diet, or lifestyle, en masse. It seems common sense to find ways of benefitting from the health attributes and flavour characteristics by including olive oil in the traditional diets of those countries. The flow-on effect could mean that olive oil is used in the restaurants in other countries where the American, Chinese and Indian cuisine is offered.

- **Flavour descriptions for multiple cuisines are not available**
  The decline of consumption of olive oil in the Mediterranean countries has forced producers and distributors to seek new markets outside the traditional importing countries. China, India, Indonesia, Russia and other populous Asian and Eastern European countries are promoted as new destinations for exports from Spain, Italy and Greece.

Recent research from the University of Nottingham's Sensory Science Centre in the United Kingdom reported that 'Asians were found to be more sensitive to sour and metallic taste than Caucasians. This is an interesting finding, as it indicates that consumers perception of taste intensity from food and beverages can be different across different ethnic groups.' The report went on to say. 'The findings from our study could help inform new product development to appeal directly to people's taste buds.' The research confirmed that there is a difference between the ability to taste and taste preferences of males and females. In research in the USA differences were also found in the taste preferences of African Americans, Hispanic Americans and non-Hispanic Americans. These and other studies have used sweetness, sourness and saltiness as the primary tastes to assess differences. In discussion about potential research projects between Savantes and the Sensory, Flavour and Consumer Science Department of the Australian research organisation CSIRO, preliminary desk research revealed 'Consumer preferences for olive oils are well established in Caucasian populations (European and North American). Limited/no studies to date have assessed olive oil preference/liking within Asian populations.' Research into the preferred flavour profiles of extra virgin olive oils of different Asian populations would seem an obvious precursor to expansion into these markets. Without this basic knowledge producers cannot tailor their blends to suit their potential consumers and would be trying to sell flavour profiles unsuitable for the customers' palate preferences.

It can be expected that the preferred flavours would be correlated to the flavour of the ingredients commonly used in consumers' traditional cuisine. Therefore, it would make good marketing sense to describe the flavours of the olive oils for these markets using the fruit, vegetal, spicy, herbal and nut ingredients used in their traditional dishes. Describing the flavours in terms of the components and ingredients of the Mediterranean diet would be meaningless. This further reinforces the folly of linking the promotion of olive oil worldwide to the promulgation of the Mediterranean diet and European lifestyle. There is much work to be done in this area if consumption in new countries is to increase rapidly.

- **Promotion and packaging do not associate the product with food**
  A visit to the International Olive Council website, front and many subsidiary pages, gives images of buildings, olive oil pouring from a bottle, table olives, olive trees, functionaries and other 'passive' images. Only when one searches the drop-down menu for 'Olive World' does one find a major reference to food under 'Recipes'. Even here the images are plates of food with no activity around them, such as families around a dining table laughing, enjoying the food with a bottle of olive oil prominent on the table with a plate of green and black table olives.

  As in the IOC mission statement where the organisation appears disconnected from the 'ordinary' people whose lives they commit to advance, promotion of olive oil seems to be disconnected from people, food and eating. If images of the consumption of olive oil are confined to the bottom of drop-down menus deep in websites or in the latter pages of publications, it should be no surprise that consumption has not increased for ten years.

The relegation of food and those consuming it with olive oil to secondary importance is not an error, or oversight, it reflects the mindset of the administrators and publicists where their activities and associates are of greater importance than increasing consumption of olive oil.

For example, many of the images submitted by Savantes and Associate Savantes for inclusion with their biographies on the Savantes website, show them with tasting glasses, tasting oil. Only two have images of the Associates enjoying food with a bottle of extra virgin olive oil on the table or being poured. This is symptomatic of the mindset of these and many other leading tasters where their skill is an end in itself, and not a means to persuade consumers to increase the consumption of olive oil in food.

Another example can be found in the images on the front pages of the 'Olive Oil World Tour' promotion funded by the Spanish Olive Oil Interprofessional and the European Union, there is no food. Pictures of olive groves tout where olive oil is born instead of pictures of happy families eating food with olive oil depicting where olive oil goes. The ubiquitous pictures are of olive oil in clear bottles – when the advice is to pack in dark bottles to eliminate the impact of light and delay oxidisation. Images are of cobalt blue tasting glasses which imply technical tasting and mean nothing to consumers. Where is the food? Where are the people, the consumers? The food is under the drop-down menu 'Make it Taste' and the images are again passive pictures of food, not active cooking and eating with happy people of all ages enjoying themselves.

These are some of the leading agencies with the responsibility of increasing the consumption of olive oil which are sending a message that their activities, the functionaries, the locations, the publications are more important than the message 'consume more olive oil'. It reflects a disconnect between the accountability to the producers who ultimately fund all activities through levies, taxes, product sales, more taxes, and political influence, and those with the responsibility of promoting increased consumption. The administration has become an end in itself, not a means to the end of expanding the industry through increasing consumption.

Perhaps this is the cause of the same approach being found along the supply chain from producers to retailers.

An internet search of olive oil brands worldwide takes one to thousands of websites promoting olive groves and their products. The front pages of the sites have images of the groves, family, processing, the mill, harvesting and the final product in bottles. Very few have images of food on the front pages, and fewer have images of food and people enjoying themselves around a table with a bottle of olive oil taking centre stage. In some way this is understandable as the producers have great pride in their work and the result. They also love using the oil in their food and should be encouraged by their leaders to show this in conjunction with their olive oil. Imagine if every time you went in search of olive oil on the internet the first images you saw on websites were happy people eating delicious food with extra virgin olive oil prominent on the table. The backdrop could be the olive grove, the people, the family, the olive oil, the brand – all covered in one active suggestive image!

When producers take their olive oils to trade shows such as the Summer Fancy Food Show in New York, the connection with food should be reinforced. If the regulations or added licences and costs preclude the offering of food for tasting with the extra virgin olive oil, the brochures and displays should feature food and culinary uses. Stopping at a stand promoting a particular brand of Greek olive oil from Crete, I asked the brand owner why the backdrop to the stand had all the compliance certifications from the local PDO to national and international quality controls, and no pictures of food and people. The answer was that the traders were more interested in certification than food. There were pictures of the grove and I respectfully refrained from asking the level of interest the traders have in olive trees. It is up to the producer primarily to accentuate the uses and flavours of the product to traders, making the certification available when required and secondary. As long as the supply chain panders to the technocrats for whom compliance is a god, the extraordinary food that is extra virgin olive oil will remain no more than another vegetable oil which needs to be constantly monitored for compliance.

The adage 'you are always marketing' should be followed. Whatever is done to sell olive oil all along the marketing chain should include the aura of extra virgin olive oil as a delicious food ingredient enjoyed by happy, healthy people.

Everything else should be seen as a secondary contributor to reinforce this message.

The exposure of olive oil to consumers is greatest in the supermarket, retail store or online shop. This is where consumers go regularly to buy their food needs. What they see on the cooking oil shelves are row upon row of cooking oils with front labels which identify the product and try and engage the shopper with a short message on the virtues of the oil. This visual display and general advertising combine with price to give the consumer the data needed to make the buying decision. Generally, in supermarkets the labels are bland with the major distinguishing feature being the brand and identifier of the contents – canola oil, olive oil, grapeseed oil. Rarely is there an evocative label with an image sending an attractive message to the consumer. The back label may carry some inducements about health benefits to the extent allowed by health claim regulations. Occasionally some notes on the flavour of the oil and food pairings can be found amongst the nutrition data on the already crowded back label.

Online stores are no different, page upon page of bottles, tasting notes and prices. Very little, if any, persuasive information or images to induce the potential customer to make olive oil their preferred ingredient. Where available such information is buried deep in drop-down menus with captions such as recipes or health benefits. If the images on the bottles, or in the pages where the bottles are displayed, showed food with healthy people, there would be no need to search the additional pages to get the message.

When I asked a leading distributor why front labels were so conformist on supermarket olive oils, the response was that that is what the consumer wants. Or is it what the consumer is used to and therefore expects? It is noticeable that slowly some innovative mainstream brands are including pictures of children, mothers cooking and even vegetables and dishes of food on the front label. These brands are starting to use the daily exposure to customers to associate the product with food, flavour, and health, all being the most important differences between extra virgin olive oil and other vegetable and seed oils. If the historical perception of olive oil is as a conservative food staple which has its place as a food ingredient in traditional Mediterranean cuisine, it is time to change this image. Images of enjoyment, foods of different cuisines, people of different ethnicities cooking, families, children, and a range of ingredients are bound to be more suggestive and alluring to customers.

Some boutique bottles of extra virgin olive are more colourful with packaging created by internationally known designers. These stand out on the shelves and attract the attention of the consumers looking for something for a special occasion, gifts when they are prepared to pay premium prices for the look of the product. Repeat purchases for everyday use will still be dependent on the flavour and quality of the product meeting their expectation. Even these upmarket designs do not portray food, even in an abstract way, being more about the artwork and bottle shape than the use of the contents.

From the producers who package the olive oil in a branded bottle or tin through to the packer or importer who purchases or imports in bulk for blending and packaging closer to the destination, the packaged oil passes through many hands, all of whom are potential consumers. For this reason all packaging, should carry images or readily assimilated messages about using olive oil. In this way the market reach will be extended to the ordinary people responsible for the handling, testing, compliance, promotion and sales of the product. In many cases, boxes used to convey olive oils to their retail destination carry the brand trademark, this can be supplemented with a message or image which will encourage consumption.

An example of a simple and appealing message from outside the olive oil industry comes with the purchase of the iconic Blundstone work boot which is famous in Australia as a durable, rugged, well-designed farming and outdoor boot. On the cardboard box in which the boot arrives and in the instructions for care are the simple words 'Everywhere Life Takes Me'. The same trademark message is on the website which also celebrates 150 years of history with the words 'our boots won't change the world, the people wearing them just might'. The olive oil industry would do well to have the same perspective on their product, 'extra virgin olive oil won't change the world, the people using it might'. The universal slogan for olive oil might be 'Everything My Body Needs'.

We need a seismic shift from the product to the people in the promotion and sale of olive oil.

Granted it is easier for a brand to deliver a single message than for a disparate competitive industry across many continents to adopt and deliver a unified message. First, there must be the leadership to promulgate the need for it, second comes the development of the message and the leadership to persuade vested interests that it is in their interests to adopt it, third, the leadership at all levels is required to persuade producers and the entire demand chain to use it consistently and continually.

- **Promotion mainly emphasises the health benefits of polyphenols and not those of the monounsaturated fat**
In the pursuit of promoting quality and avoiding many of the managerial problems caused by disease, pestilence and the weather in groves where olives are late harvested, and to overcome the problems of oxidisation during distribution to the consumer, polyphenols or antioxidants are the central focus of many promotions of extra virgin olive oils. They impart flavour and research indicates are active in the prevention or mitigation of many diseases. They are a small proportion, 1-3%, of the chemical make-up of extra virgin olive oil which sets the product apart from other vegetable oils which, even if cold pressed and unrefined, do not have the same flavours or stability imparted by antioxidants. However, these can be added to vegetable oils by blending with olive oil or using plant extracts.

Approximately 56-75% of olive oil, refined or extra virgin, comprises monounsaturated fat which is deemed to be healthier than polyunsaturated or saturated fats found in vegetable oils and animal fats. Two exceptions are canola oil and avocado oil, especially the high oleic canola oil, which have levels of monounsaturated fats equal to olive oil. This health benefit and stabilising effect is often overshadowed by the promotion of the polyphenol antioxidants in olive oil. It is in the interest of increased consumption of olive oil that refined olive oil, despite having a low level of polyphenols, is also promoted as being a healthy and relatively stable product. The point of difference with mainstream vegetable oils is that it is not solvent extracted prior to refining, a benefit when there is fear of the alleged carcinogenic effect of some solvents.

Promoting the solvent free and health benefits of refined olive oil which is available at a cheaper price than extra virgin olive oil gives an entry point. This move by consumers to garner some of the health benefits may lead to the use of extra virgin olive oil in the future. The step-by-step approach may be appropriate for young people who cannot afford extra virgin or those who are not brought up to appreciate its strong flavour. The first step will be to use a blend of the preferred vegetable oil with refined olive oil, then refined olive oil, a step up in price and taste will be refined olive oil blended with extra virgin and ultimately extra virgin olive oil. This incremental persuasion for consumers to commit to full use of one or all of the classifications of olive oil will cast a wider net and be inclusive rather than exclusive. Currently, across the industry, afficionados frown upon the use of any olive oil other than extra virgin. While they may ply their trade through the sale of the product or services surrounding it, they do a disservice to themselves and the industry at large by limiting its growth, and thereby limiting the growth of their enterprises.

Showing Respect for People and Products

- **Producing regions do not show respect for the olive oil products from other regions and countries**
  One of the strategies of the IOC is *'Enabling government representatives and experts to meet regularly to discuss problems and concerns and to fix priorities for IOC action.'* Discounting the negative approach this implies by not including 'opportunities', the achievement of this aim should foster a mutual respect for the production of other countries, the sum of which makes up the global industry. This respect should filter down in the countries represented and encourage an international cohesive approach to the promotion of olive oil.

  Unfortunately, too often the politics of international competition mean that representatives seeking election take the populist approach of denigrating production from other countries. A presentation of Mario Solinas Quality Award winning oils from Spain, Italy and Greece to some members of Congress, aides and media in Washington serves as an example. During negative publicity about the quality of olive oil coming from Europe the diplomats charged with promoting agricultural products from the European Union convened the meeting. Approximately 50 influential members of the House of Representatives, aides and Washington media assembled to hear presentations by representatives from each country and participate in a tasting presented by the author, who being from Australia, was deemed sufficiently independent to show no favour.

  It can be assumed that the quality and flavour profile of the olive oils was of a very high standard, being the winners of the most rigorous competition in the world under the auspices of the International Olive Council. Diplomatically there was one oil from each of the three countries and at no stage were the relative competition scores or placing revealed.

The verbal presentations given by the representatives from each country were more appropriate for an audience of academics or scientists, too technical for the policy makers who would normally defer to scientific and other advisers for technical advice. There were also comments during the presentations, and after the tasting, which revealed the personal preferences of the regional representatives showing the lack of unity and respect for the preferences of others. The result was an opportunity missed to present a united front, each country praising the quality of the extra virgin olive oils of excellence being tasted and emphasising that the variations in intensity and of flavours suited a wide range of palates and preferences. Personal preferences and regional bias should have no place when presenting a product on behalf of an industry or trading block.

The self-imposed imperative to be seen to be unbiased in presentation of olive oils from different regions contributes to the IOC ceding much of the responsibility for marketing to the producing countries. There is care in not identifying brands using only generic varieties in tastings.

It would be in the interest of the overall industry for the IOC to remove this straight-jacket and encourage activities which exchange products from different regions and bring together groups such as panels, producers and administrators with the express intent of learning about the industries in different countries and building international networks to foster respect.

At the same time, those representing producing regions in other countries should frame their comments and presentations in terms which show respect for all extra virgin olive oils while emphasising the points of difference where relevant. Even within one's own territory, regard should be given to the rapid dissemination of any comments through social media and comments should be couched in respectful terms. The uttering of leaders sets the tone of the thinking of their followers.

- **There is a lot of publicity about fraudulent olive oil**
  Olive oil ranks among the top ten most fraudulent foods and is frequently ranked first in fraud by some agencies. Paradoxically, it is one of the most regulated foods. One would expect that being so regulated with a long list of quality specifications would assure the consumer is receiving the genuine product.

  Fraud is defined as 'wrongful or criminal deception intended to result in financial or personal gain'. It is the 'intentional deception' which is frequently disregarded by journalists or commentators reporting on a testing programme which has detected olive oils which do not meet the International Olive Council Trade Standards. Sometimes the word fraud is used intentionally to grab headlines when one product is trying to discredit another.

  Olive oil does have a long history of adulteration and fraud perpetrated by international criminal brotherhoods intent on political and financial gain. There are books written about this activity which imply that it is pervasive in the industry. There are from time-to-time reports of the police in European countries making arrests connected with trade in adulterated olive oil. When analysed, the quantities involved in these criminal activities are relatively small and insignificant in an industry which sells three million tonnes of olive oil each year. Where arrests aren't made it is fair to assume any allegations are hearsay. The implication of this is that the criminal activity is given far more publicity than it warrants, perhaps by those who will gain by discrediting olive oil and getting their vegetable oil into the market. Electronic and social media also amplify one incident well beyond its importance by rapidly transmitting it worldwide and recording its repetition in media which has significant following. An arrest in Italy involving a container of olive oil alleged to be fraudulent may involve 20 tonnes of olive oil. It is reported and magnified by those who want to be seen to be doing their jobs, by those who wish to discredit the Italian production, and by those who want to undermine the integrity of olive oil. In no time this incident which may involve olive oil with a retail value of 100,000 Euros, or the price of two upmarket cars, has been publicised worldwide and added fuel to the olive oil fraud bandwagons.

  In an attempt to assure customers of the integrity of olive oil the industry has imposed layer upon layer of compliance. It is a truism that the more regulations with which a product must comply, the more chances there are of non-compliance. Perhaps the problem of alleged fraud is not one which will be remedied by more regulation, the remedy may be more effective policing.

The intentional act of fraud by adulteration or substitution is the responsibility of police or appointed agencies to detect and eliminate. Inadvertent, unintentional, contamination can take place in refining and other facilities where quality control processes are inadequate, equipment failure or human error causes mixing of oils. This is not fraud unless the trader knowingly sells the contaminated product under the wrong classification.

Olive oil and other vegetable oils degrade over time to become rancid through oxidation. Once the olive oil leaves the producer in pristine condition it is handled by many traders before it reaches the consumer. Along the way, adverse storage or transport conditions can compromise the oil and result in rancidity. The olive oil may be presented to the consumer labelled as extra virgin and when tested shown to be rancid. This is only fraud if the retailer knows it is rancid and does not meet the specification on the label. If the retailer does not know the product is defective and has the paperwork from the supplier showing compliance, it is a matter for consumer protection agencies to investigate and apply a sanction which is unlikely to be a criminal conviction. The latter case is more an example of ignorance than fraud.

An examination of sources of alleged fraud will show that much of the gossip is just that, hearsay generated by the prospect of financial gain or personal status.

It is common to hear a local producer criticise the product of their neighbour or a competitor in the local area. This is most often unjustified and done for personal gain in reputation or sales. It may be the manifestation of a long running feud. Whatever the reason, it is the seat of many allegations of deception or 'fraud'.

From the local level, the next example of contrived circumstances to reveal fraud by producers is the testing of samples by producer associations to denigrate competing products and promote those of their members. This 'predatory testing' may be accompanied by introducing a set of additional standards which favour locally produced products at the expense of imported products. Testing is then done to the new standard and oils which do not comply are tagged as fraudulent in publicity, even when they meet the internationally accepted trade standard. If the association has a quality ‘seal’ it has been known that threats are made publicly that those products which do not carry the seal will be targeted for testing in an apparent attempt to coerce the brand to join the association quality programme. The testing programmes are sometimes financed by enterprises which will potentially gain market share from publicising the alleged fraud of competitors. When these instances have been pursued by consumer protection agencies or class actions, the lack of rigour of the protocols of collecting samples and testing have generally resulted in the investigations or actions being dropped.

There are occasional claims of fraudulent sale of non-compliant olive oil on social media posts from tasters certified by tasting short courses. These self-appointed ‘vigilantes’ claim to buy and taste mainly supermarket olive oils and deem them rancid and imply fraudulent sales by the brand and retailer. These tasters defy the international trade standard requirement that the samples and tastings be undertaken following certain protocols including the requirement of a minimum of eight tasters in an accredited tasting panel. There seems to be no justification other than personal aggrandisement for the tasters from these activities which can have substantial financial consequences for the brand and retailer.

Consumer magazines frequently undertake evaluation of products bought off the shelf at retailers. Olive oil is regularly a subject of these investigations with the results being published online and in magazines. The degree of rigour of these assessments is varied with evaluating panels ranging from trained accredited tasters in a full panel to a small select group of ‘celebrity’ tasters known to the magazine. The degree of adherence to protocols covering sample selection and storage is not always revealed and any claims of defective product are not double checked. The positive impact on the sales of the favoured products in these articles is substantial, as is the depressing effect on the sales of the alleged defective products. It is rarely in the interest of the suppliers of the discredited product to challenge the findings because of cost and the increase in negative publicity caused by legal action.

The same lack of rigour is shown by some international olive oil competitions which do not have specific quality criteria for entry. In 2015 at the New York

International Olive Oil Competition (NYIOOC) which claims on its website to be 'the largest and most prestigious olive oil quality contest' the convenors reported that of the 671 olive oils which competed, 49% had been judged defective by the international panel of expert judges after 'three days of hard work'. Given the cost of entry and couriering of the samples it is unlikely that producers would waste their money by sending defective oils. It would also be expected that any entries would be accompanied by the necessary certification to prove the olive oil had been classified as extra virgin. This requirement would save the judges tasting many defective oils and wasting their time. The downside for the organisers is that the introduction of strict entry requirements would increase the cost of entry and most likely considerably reduce the income from entries.

A question must be asked of the judges as to their willingness to judge in a competition where there is no guarantee that the winning oils are extra virgin. They may meet the flavour requirements, but the lack of chemical testing may let some non-compliant oils through.

The claim that so many of the entries were deemed defective by a panel which had no authority to classify the oils is very damaging to the industry as it tends to reinforce the perception of the consuming public that there is a high prevalence of sub-standard and possibly fraudulent olive oil on the market. It is noticeable that this competition no longer publicises the percentage of olive oils deemed defective in subsequent competitions.

This is an example where an influential activity can have an impact on the image of the industry through adopting processes which are about maximising the financial advantage to the organisers, while being less than rigorous in the treatment of the product which they set themselves up to judge.

The approach by the IOC to encourage the detection and definition of defects first in the official tasting process must bear some responsibility for this emphasis on fraud. If their approach was that positive flavours should be identified first it could change the approach of the whole industry and consign fraud and the sale of defective oil to its rightful place as a small volume in an industry which overwhelmingly controls the quality of its product.

In February 2016 the global media company Forbes published an article with the caption 'The Olive Oil Scam: If 80% Is Fake, Why Do You Keep Buying It?' The opening paragraphs continued 'It's reliably reported that 80% of the Italian olive oil on the market is fraudulent. Some experts think that percentage is an exaggeration. Others believe that the bigger problem is poor quality olive oil, deliberately mislabelled as virgin or extra virgin. In any case, it's likely that when you buy olive oil, you're not buying what it says on the label.'

The article refers to a warning in the New York Times which allegedly states, 'Much of the Italian extra virgin olive oil flooding the world's market shelves is neither Italian nor virgin'.

There are assertions in these articles from media outlets with a substantial worldwide following. There appears to be no rebuttal from Italian industry organisations or from the International Olive Council. With modern media watch capabilities, it would be possible to respond to these media articles almost immediately, but there seems to be nothing. In its efforts to promote quality and combat fraud, counteracting this damaging publicity should be a priority for the IOC. Silence seems to condone on these occasions.

- **Consumers do not trust the integrity of the olive oil**
  With the publicity given to fraud and alleged scams relating to olive oil it is not surprising that consumers have doubts about the integrity of the olive oil they buy. Somehow the effort to reassure consumers that they are getting the product described on the label reinforces that they should be wary.

  The industry needs to change its own attitude and portray confidence in the integrity of its product and let others prove otherwise. This must occur at all levels of the industry and be led by a slogan sending a message with which everyone can identify. A message which transcends the parochial regional interests of olive oil producers thereby uniting them in the cause to convince consumers of the integrity of the olive oil product they purchase.

  A campaign must be mounted to involve producers and traders locally, regionally, nationally and internationally. To achieve this will take leadership at national and international level which has not been evident in the 10 years of no growth in olive oil consumption. When the industry has its messaging positive and active, the loyal consumers of olive oil can be encouraged to be advocates through promotional schemes which extend a benefit to them. Many such schemes exist in other industries where there is a reward if you refer a friend. It is time the olive oil industry modernised its sales activities.

The industry at all levels must take responsibility for the product delivered to consumers and expose and publicly condemn instances of proven fraud or activities which seek to discredit competing products for gain. The cavalier approach by some new entrants who are not concerned about the damage they do to the industry as long as they gain increased market share, should be challenged, exposed and condemned.

Beware of Competition from Vegetable Oils

- **Competing vegetable oils are mimicking the profile of olive oil with associated health benefits**
  Research indicates that olive oil, especially extra virgin, is active in preventing and mitigating many diseases and chronic illnesses. Some of the health benefits are attributed to the high level of monounsaturated (oleic) fatty acids and vitamins in the oil fraction and others to the polyphenol antioxidants which impart the flavour.

  The health benefits of olive oil occupy much of the promotion and publicity space devoted to products, often in combination with the promotion of the Mediterranean diet.

  The effectiveness of the promotion of health benefits and higher prices for other 'healthy' vegetable oils has resulted in the breeding or engineering of high oleic acid canola, or rapeseed, oil with high a monounsaturated fatty acid level approaching that of olive oil. High oleic soybean oil and sunflower oils are also widely available in the market.

  Avocado oil is a relatively new entry into the market with production ramping up in Mexico. Apart from the polyphenol component, avocado oil has a fat profile very similar to olive oil with a higher smoke point. The brand name Olivado adopted by a New Zealand avocado oil product clearly promotes the similarities with olive oil seen as a positive to consumers.

The price difference between these high oleic products and olive oil makes them a serious contender for the 'healthy' cooking oil market. Consequently, the additional benefits of olive oil, the natural production process and flavour will become more prevalent in promotion.

- **The smoke point of extra virgin olive oil is perceived to be low**
  The smoke point of olive oil is frequently raised as a reason for choosing other vegetable oils for cooking, especially in the USA and other non-Mediterranean countries. Chefs and home cooks in the main producing regions use olive oil throughout their cooking with no fear of the toxic substances which, some claim, are produced when it is used at high temperatures. All vegetable oils and animal fats 'burn' if used at unusually high temperatures in cooking resulting in a range of potentially toxic substances as the fat breaks down.

  A lot of energy and airtime is spent defending the olive oil smoke point in the USA where it has been used effectively by marketers of competing oils to discourage its use.

  When compared with the smoke points of most refined vegetable oils, refined olive oil compares favourably and can be used in place of them for most cooking. Extra virgin olive oil has a lower smoke point than refined oils but the antioxidants in more robust products raise the smoke point to levels acceptable for most home cooking. Most extra virgin olive oils have smoke points around 187°C, well above the normal frying pan temperature of 180°C. The conclusion is that olive oil, either refined or extra virgin, is appropriate for use in all cooking.

  The continuing and frequent defence against the perceived adverse publicity about smoke point in the USA only serves to keep the issues at the front of the mind of consumers. Constant promotion of the use of olive oil for all cooking, without reference to smoke point, will in time diminish the impact of negative publicity.

- **Blending**
  When the Australian wool market collapsed following the overproduction and high price of fine wool used for clothing at the high-end of the market, it had another option. Rather than being the fibre used for its length and strength for cloth used in expensive male and female clothing, it could have been sold as a

high value but relatively small component of strong fibre blends for socks or underwear, or some other everyday garment. This may have precluded the investment by manufacturers in developing an artificial fibre with the length and strength of fine wool, or at least delayed it until the fine wool stockpile had been sold at a reasonable price.

Observers of the Spanish olive oil industry will note some similarities with the current situation of olive oil production in Spain. Good prices have encouraged the establishment of many new mechanised groves which have increased production. On the demand side the consumption of olive oil has not increased in 10 years and has declined in Spain. The application of tariffs by the USA on Spanish packaged olive oil in retribution for the subsidies for Airbus from the European Union has exacerbated the situation. Overlay the Covid-19 pandemic and its impact on household disposable income, the olive oil industry was in a state of overproduction with carryover stocks currently three times normal and approximately equal to 30% of annual production. Then came the war in Ukraine which affected the supply of other vegetable oils and the devastating drought in Spain which it is estimated will reduce olive oil production by over 40%. The price of extra virgin olive oil rose in line with threats to supply and increasing demand. When this situation passes and there is a return to normality of production in Spain and the supply of vegetable oils returns as other countries increase production, one can expect trading of olive oil at reasonable prices for the consumer will resume. The decrease in supply can be expected to affect consumption globally and the cost-of-living squeeze may also reduce consumers' purchases of the more expensive extra virgin olive oils.

The Spanish industry representatives appear to be mainly from the larger producers with their main interest being producing and maintaining the price for extra virgin olive oil. The Spanish government in response has advocated the early harvesting of olives to produce a lower yield and higher quality extra virgin olive oil. Not only will this produce a lower volume of olive oil, but also result in the oils having a longer shelf-life, effectively giving the option to carry the stocks forward. The government has also introduced a system of storage of lower grade lampante olive oil to remove it from the market and maintain the higher price. This move has again shifted the sell down of stocks to the future.

It is little solace to the smaller producers of boutique oil from traditional groves that there is talk of promoting the purchase of extra virgin olive oil from these groves by identifying the origin on the bottle and mounting a publicity campaign to encourage consumers to buy in sympathy with the small producers. Given the multitude of competing promotions on quality it is unlikely that consumers will be persuaded, especially if the price of the boutique olive oils is higher than the oil produced from super high- density plantations with the claim that their product is of equal quality.

By interfering in the market by withdrawing supply to maintain steady demand and higher prices, the olive oil industry is arguably making the same mistake as the Australian wool industry. Producers putting a higher price on their product than consumers are willing to pay because of some perceived intrinsic value is naïve. The belief that controlling supply to maintain prices because the country is the largest producer also ignores the fact that other countries such as Tunisia and Turkey are supplying increasing volumes, as are new world producers. Letting the market play out without interference gives price signals of what consumers are prepared to pay and sets olive oil and extra virgin olive oil realistically in the hierarchy of preference for vegetable oils. The effort to maintain higher value will then be directed to innovation and differentiation rather than control of supply.

One of the options is to market high value high polyphenol extra virgin olive oil as a health and flavour additive for other vegetable and seed oils. Avocado oil and high oleic acid seed oils such as soybean and canola oil are so often deemed the enemies of olive oil. They should be seen as allies in the pursuit of increased consumption of vegetable oils rather than animal fats. Extra virgin olive oil can provide additional health benefits and flavour when blended with vegetable oils at levels of anywhere from 5% to 25% of the blend. The benefit to the olive industry will be to be a small and high-value proportion of a massively larger market. Currently olive oil is around 1.5% of world vegetable oil consumption, if blending can lift this to 3% the industry would double its market share 'piggy-backing' on the well-resourced international seed and vegetable oil market. For example, the corn oil and avocado oil producers in the USA would become the allies of extra virgin olive oil producers who provide a flavouring and health component to their product.

Other initiatives to maintain the price of extra virgin and refined olive oil which could be boosted are those directed towards extracting high-value components such as squalene and oleocanthal and using the 'depleted' olive oil for manufacturing or energy production as a biofuel. Squalene is a component of some adjuvants used to enhance the immune response of some vaccines – topical now with the response to the Covid-19 pandemic. The industry must pursue alternative uses as a contingency while maintaining the core market as a food ingredient. This diversity of options will be more effective in maintaining higher prices in the long term than withdrawing supply of a product which degrades and loses value in storage. The maintenance of higher prices will be more effective than conversion of traditional groves to super high-density production in maintaining the socio-economic well-being of small producers. As previously stated, the percentage of traditionally planted Spanish groves which can be converted to high-density with associated mechanisation is below 50% with the limiting factors being terrain and water availability.

Popular amongst some consumers, especially in the USA with their propensity to buy ready-made products, are the 'infused' olive oils. Infusion with herbs and spices such as garlic, chilli or rosemary is another form of blending. In some of the oil and vinegar stores popular in the shopping malls in the USA the sale of infused olive oil far outstrips the sale of extra virgin olive oils.

The Business of Flavour

While you are waiting for your grove to grow and the first harvest is in sight, your exploration of the complex world of olive oil may leave you perplexed and wondering where your product will fit. If you have bought an established grove your first harvest will be imminent. Whatever the situation the basic principles of production, processing and marketing apply.

Management Style

There are aspects which you can control, those you can influence to a greater or lesser degree and those over which you have no control. If you optimise the management of the controllable, are active in the areas you can influence and keep aware of the influences you cannot control you should have a thriving enterprise. The word optimise is used instead of maximise to suggest that maximising everything all the time may increase the managerial and financial risk of your enterprise. A grove which controls input costs and accepts production below that expected if inputs are maximised may be a better prospect to weather the vagaries of the environment and markets. Diversity of products is another way of spreading the risk of fluctuating demand and variable seasons.

Technical advice on how to manage your trees is readily available from established groves, associations, the internet and service providers. There will be a divergence between the advice provided by the long-established groves and the new modern groves. Unsurprisingly, there are many traditional methods in the older growing regions which make the farmers shake their heads at the new modern super high-density groves. These practices vary considerably from region to region, for example, pruning and tree shape in Italian groves is quite different from the Spanish groves. These have developed through a combination of science, availability of labour and style of product. All are supported by research from local universities and government research institutes. That they work is evident by the almost universal adoption in the localities. However, this does not mean that they are the best practice with conservatism, peer pressure and other social interaction tending to make operators conform. If your new grove is in such a locality, be prepared to have shaking heads and even political pressure if you dare to try something new, for example, plant a Spanish variety in a grove in Tuscany. Locals do not like outsiders breezing in with money and new ideas which upset their peaceful agrarian equilibrium.

In new growing regions it is easier to select the practices which seem to be most compatible with the aims of the enterprise and the varieties planted. Recognition of the background of those providing advice is important as the information will probably emanate from the region where the advisers acquired their experience. A simple rule to follow is to seek the advice of those from the region where the varieties originate, southern Spain for picual, Catalunya for arbequina, Greece for koroneiki, Puglia in Italy for coratina and so on. Not only have the trees been selected and bred to suit the agronomic conditions in those regions, but the management practices have also been adapted to suit the trees. The nuances go beyond the horticulture to the ease of extraction of the oil, extraction from picual coming from dry climates where moisture content of the olive is usually low, becomes difficult when the moisture content is high.

Olive trees are living beings and cannot be manipulated like some mechanical device, adding here and subtracting there. The trees' resilience, despite some abuses perpetrated by humans over centuries, is testament to their tolerance and adaptability. The management of the trees can be likened to an assembly line with automated actions driven by computers or to an assembly of individuals with different characters and needs. In the former case the grove can be managed remotely from a home or office with automated irrigation controlled by computers over the internet responding to soil moisture meters. Pruning is mechanical, the tree getting trimmed top and sides in a military haircut and harvesting is also mechanical with timing determined by laboratories using oil accumulation measurement supplemented with measurement of biophenols and moisture content. If the moisture is too high the computers will reduce water application. Insect traps monitor the infestations and occasional inspection assesses fungal diseases. Application of herbicides, fungicides and pesticides is automated. Towers with wind vanes are switched on when the temperature drops to frost levels and the air is circulated to reduce frost damage. The whole operation is a production line to maximise output. Capital input is also maximised, and insurance to some extent will offset risk. Enterprises managed in this way are at the forefront of olive oil production and of necessity new groves taking this approach must be large to generate the income to give a return on the substantial capital investment. They are the domain of large corporations and venture capital. They are not always successful, forcing mergers, takeovers, recapitalisation and insolvency in some cases.

At the other end of the scale are the small, generally family-owned, groves where the trees are tended individually and capital investment limited to that required for essentials. The advantage of working one's own grove is the daily observation of the trees and familiarity with their behaviour which indicates their well-being or otherwise. The olive tree has an extraordinary ability to adjust its growth and productivity to suit the growing conditions. If the soil is fertile and water abundant, the tree will grow vegetatively often producing little or no fruit, as if there is no need to procreate because life is pretty good. Stress the tree by controlling the water and the apparent need to procreate results in a heavy fruit load. Giving the tree a lot of water as it emerges from the autumn/winter fruiting season and looks to the next 'breeding' period will give the message that water will be abundant for the coming summer and the tree will set a heavy fruit load thereby requiring a lot of water when it is in short supply in summer. When the tree is short of water in summer it will shed leaves to reduce transpiration and save the fruit. If water is still limiting, some fruit will start to be selectively denied nutrients and shrivel while others will be allowed to continue growth. Heavy pruning will result in sucker growth as the tree uses the root system developed to support a large vegetative canopy. The tree lives and adjusts to its environment, the art of management is to read the signs and provide an environment most conducive to the level of production required.

Between the extremes of the very traditional small family groves and the super high-density plantations there is every combination of size and management. All have their place, and all can be viable if managed optimally. In our grove we have opted for minimal use of mechanisation and maximum use of personal observation achieved by doing the work in the grove ourselves. This means a compromise in yields and income. Risk is minimised with very direct management and few external inputs. The olive enterprise is supplemented with income from Savantes activities and consulting.

The choice on the management style is yours. The size of the grove will dictate the running costs and the efficient management of the trees the income. Between planting and the first harvest the grove management is confined to tree training through pruning, pest and disease management, weed control and irrigation.

The First Harvest

Assuming you have established a new grove, the trees have been growing and tended for a few years. If you have bought an established grove the following suggestion still applies a little bit earlier in the ownership. The first annual harvest is imminent, and it is time to make decisions about selling the first olive oil. While managing the grove to this stage, your research has apprised you of the world of olive oil trade you are about to enter. It may seem daunting and complex; however, it offers a world of opportunity for those with the knowledge and courage to exploit the opportunities and manage a brand profitably.

There will be palpable excitement at the prospect of the first harvest and the taste of the first extra virgin olive produced from the grove. Of course, it is going to be the best extra virgin olive oil ever produced and worth every cent a customer pays. Enjoy the excitement then moderate your expectation of sales and take a realistic pragmatic approach.

In the lead up to harvest as the olives ripen take representative samples from the different varieties and send them to a selected laboratory for testing for the olive oil percentage and moisture content. The olives ripen from green to a straw colour, then start darkening and eventually turn completely purple or black. Keep records of everything you do, they will help immensely in decision making in future years. The camera on your phone is a useful tool to record the stage of ripeness of the samples you send off to the laboratory for oil accumulation and moisture testing. When you get the results file them with the pictures. Make a graph of the increase in oil accumulation in weekly intervals and if you are having the polyphenol level tested, this can be on the graph as well. Moisture content will fluctuate depending on the uncontrolled precipitation from rain and the controlled application of irrigation water. If you can afford the cost of weekly testing for each variety your data set will be more comprehensive for decisions on harvest timing. If this is too costly take a representative sample across the varieties. Oil accumulation will vary with the season and should be recorded along with the daily weather conditions. In time the acquired knowledge will help make management decisions even if the full testing regime is discontinued. When making decisions, laboratory generated data should be tempered with acquired knowledge of the behaviour of the trees and the product the market requires.

As the olives ripen the oil content will increase and the polyphenol level decline. Advice can be sought as to the optimal harvest timing to give you the oil profile you are aiming at – more robust with less oil with high polyphenols and more delicate with more oil with lower polyphenols. Ideally in the initial stages if you have your own processor or have enough from each variety to have small batches processed you should experiment with harvest timing for each variety giving you a range of intensities and oil yields. This will be most informative but likely to be managerially difficult and expensive. The pressure will be to harvest early and get robust high polyphenol oils, thereby avoiding frost damage and fungal diseases. Most of the grove can be managed this way with a small part harvested later to give an idea of the risks and results from a flavour and oil yield perspective. This knowledge will be valuable if at some later stage you wish to change the flavour profile of your product.

Selling The First Oil

The temptation with your first harvest is to sell it all, quickly. Assuming you have the olives processed to extract the oil, this will involve selecting the packaging, designing labels, acquiring boxes for distribution and looking for distribution and outlets. It is time for caution and to channel the excitement into a planned entry into the market. Where and how are you going to sell your extra virgin olive oil?

There are some principles of supply which should be considered when making this decision:

- Reliability
- Consistency
- Quality
- Flexibility
- Price

The first, the reliability of supply, is critical whichever channel you choose to sell your product, especially food service (Horeca) and retail. If you sell to a trader, the continuity and consistency of supply in bulk is less important as they in many cases spot buy small volumes, dependent on quality and price. The oil may be blended or traded unchanged to a specific market. The number of harvests the contract covers with the trader will indicate the importance of the oil to their trading. It is unlikely with a first harvest that the volume will be great enough to interest traders with anything more than a one-off sale. However, it may be worth taking some samples to a few traders to get an opinion, indication of volume required and price, and to put yourself on their list of potential suppliers. The opinion of traders is probably more objective than friends, family, associations and competition judges as it assesses your product in the real world of trading olive oil for profit.

Reliability is very important wherever you sell your oil, simply because if supply runs out all the effort in promotion by you, the distributor and retailer is wasted when a converted customer comes to make a purchase and it is sold out. The boast that 'we have sold out everything' may impress some but not those who understand the dynamics of the retail market which demands that continuity of supply is critical to retaining and growing a customer base. If your product is not there the retailer will replace it and most likely terminate the supply agreement. Customers will turn to the replacement or some other product. Early in the production it is critical that you do not overreach in the number of channels and outlets your supply, ensuring that you can supply until the new harvest is bottled and ready for delivery.

The channels available to you are diverse, starting with selling to friends or, if you are connected to agritourism, to visitors. You can sell online which is a good way to maintain availability to friends and visitors without the hassle of intermittent delivery of small volumes, associated invoicing and follow-up on payment which is always a sensitive issue with friends.

Farmer and food markets are an outlet for many small producers. These involve considerable travel and usually consume weekends. The advantage is that the costs are low and contact with the customers is very direct. Those who buy food at these markets are usually discerning on quality and prepared to pay a little more. Beware of selling your product at the markets for more or less than it is available at other retail outlets in the area. Undercutting your wholesale customers will affect their sales and charging more than they do in their retail outlets will undermine your sales at the market. Consistency of price setting is as important as the consistency of supply. Understand that everyone in the supply chain must make a profit to trade in your product. It is common for a distributor to add 100% to the price they pay, and the retailer another 100% on the price from the distributor. This may of course vary depending on the style of the shop, the turnover and other considerations. As the producer, one should be aware of the selling prices at all stages, you will learn that it is not wise to comment to the vendor and suggest prices unless asked, it is their business and setting the price is their prerogative. Many producers try to cut out the distributors and go direct to the retailer. Realistic costing of one's time and travel in servicing multiple customers, invoicing and credit control, and comparative turnover will often show that using a distributor is more cost-effective. Here again, it is important to understand the distributor's expectation on the use of other distributors for the same product. Be open with those you supply, inform them of any changes in the product, for example a new harvest being delivered, and give them any tips on marketing or selling which will help them move your product.

Early on in selling, producers will quickly learn that having a range of products amortises the costs of selling over a broader base and the chance of having something that attracts a customer is greater. The objective at a market is to attract a customer to the stand, once achieved the 'sell' should follow. Providing only one intensity of an extra virgin olive oil is less likely to result in sales than offering a delicate, medium and robust option. Olive oil consumers have their preferences and as so often happens, trying to persuade them, or 'educate' them, that a robust oil is what they should buy may turn them away. Give them a taste, preferably in food, and let them decide. Proselytising the merits of robust olive oils and associated health benefits has its place, but not at a market where time should be devoted to transactions. The same goes for trade and food shows.

Whether you start with the markets, a distributor, retailer, or a restaurant, having a range of olive oils gives options and a broader 'face' on retail shelves. Knowing the flavour profiles of each product, uses in food and having supporting quality documentation and brochures adds another impressive level to your sales pitch. Many like a story which will give substance or soul to your product – especially to sections of consumers who have an environmental and organic ethos.

Research your target market before making the appointment to sell your product. Check the business website and the range of products and prices. Go into the retail store and look at the display, identify competing products and their sales pitch, note the prices, look at the harvest dates of the olive oils, taste those on offer and work out how your product compares. Go to lunch or dinner at the restaurant, study the menu, inquire about the olive oil used, note the cuisine and anything else which will give you a marketing edge when you go in to sell your olive oil products. Chefs are busy, usually take Monday off and restaurants have little storage space. They often change their menus to accommodate seasonal produce, these regular menu changes may be an opportunity to persuade them to try a different extra virgin olive oil. Find out the packaging preferences, glass in commercial kitchens can be a food safety problem, taps on larger containers make it easier for cooks to decant the oil. All these location and trade specific details give the salesperson knowledge which will make a sale more achievable.

When the time for the sales appointment arrives, take the inquisitive approach. Discreetly find out how much the customer knows about olive oil and adjust your pitch accordingly. If talking to a chef, ask whether they use olive oil, which classification and in what food. Do they have a preferred flavour profile and how much do they use? If they offer you a taste of the oil they use, don't choke on it even if it is in your view not up to the quality of yours. Don't say it is defective, if it is rancid, or you think it is, a taste of your oils should provide a better flavour profile in contrast. Olive oil users do not like to be told that the product they are using is of poor quality, it is a challenge to their professionalism.

If taking a sample, always taste a bottle from the same batch before setting out. On many occasions on Savantes courses and less formal meetings, producers or salespeople have given me an oil to taste which is without doubt rancid. This tells me two things; their quality control is poor and don't buy their oil. On one occasion a very good taster presented a sample of their extra virgin olive oil for use in one of the meals at an international conference. Always checking any product we use we decided that this was rancid, and he agreed. He had taken it off the sample shelf at work without checking. The same applies if someone else gives you a sample to take, make sure the quality is as described on the label. Good tasters never forget the brand of a substandard extra virgin or other olive oil, they may not talk about it but will not forget it.

Be prepared to correct any misconceptions about olive oil, for example the smoke point precluding its use in cooking. This requires knowledge of the smoke point of competing vegetable oils. Knowledge about competing cooking oils and fats will help you persuade a customer that it is in their interest to use olive oil. Often the price difference is a hurdle, so you need to suggest a way of the purchaser recovering the increased price by way of advertising healthier food or the like. Perhaps offer a blend of olive oil with another vegetable oil as a cheaper first step towards conversion.

When in New York presenting the Savantes courses I always stay at the same hotel in the Hell's Kitchen area. At the end of the course there are always many opened bottles of olive oil which I give to the staff. In successive years I had the same staff member servicing my room. The first year she selected a Uruguayan extra virgin olive oil. The second year, when asked to select her preference from the array of opened bottles, she again selected the Uruguayan brand. I asked her if the intensity was to her liking, her response was that it was too strong for her taste, but she blended it with 50% corn oil and it was perfect! She was half converted!

Retailers place their olive oils on shelves, chefs use them in the kitchen and in some cases like to place branded bottles on the diner's table. In other restaurants olive oil is decanted into containers, usually clear glass, and placed on the table. Frequently these bottles and containers are refilled or topped up without the containers being thoroughly washed. The result is that the oil goes rancid and the top up with fresh oil just increases the amount of rancid oil. If the branded bottle is yours, this practice may well give your olive oil a bad name. In extreme cases the branded bottles are filled with a cheaper lower quality oil. In Europe legislation that bans this practice and dictates that extra virgin olive oil be sold in non-refillable bottles has gone some way to stopping this dishonest practice.

Many of these issues occurring in food service and some retailers come from lack of knowledge on how to store and use extra virgin olive oil. Factsheets and offers to train staff are useful add-ons to selling your brand.

When I started selling our first harvest of olive oil, I made most of the mistakes mentioned above. Very pleased with my newly acquired knowledge about the excellence of locally produced extra virgin olive and armed with our first bottles from the grove I blundered into restaurants and basically told the chefs that the oil they were using was rubbish and they should use ours. I never made a sale and chastened, talked to some friends in the food media, took their advice and then changed the way I went about approaching new customers. I understood that many in foodservice have long-standing relationships with their suppliers and any change would only come about by building relationships and waiting for the opportunity to supply a product. This opportunity may arise when a chef decides to present a menu of local foods and needs a locally produced olive oil to compliment the menu rather than the imported one hitherto used. The menu may require an oil or oils of particular flavour profiles and with your tasting ability you may be able to blend to that requirement.

Having worked out the volume you can supply, selected the channels you can service with product, and convinced your customers of your knowledge underpinning the quality and integrity of your olive oil, it is time to deliver. Then, hopefully, repeat orders follow as your product gains market share. Consumers will buy the product for a range of reasons; flavour, region, packaging, price and many more. They expect that the product will be the same whenever and wherever they buy it, they expect consistency. Here your knowledge of the flavour profile of the oils from different varieties in your grove and ability to blend will help in keeping consistent blends year in year out. A customer does not want to buy a brand of olive oil which they are used to as delicate intensity, to suddenly find that the contents of the usual bottle has become robust because there is a change in supply. They will look for a new brand and the confidence in the original brand is lost, probably forever. The packaging should also be consistent for instant recognition, changing design or bottles can result in similar loss of customers who do not have the time to look for the changed presentation.

Packaging and Presentation

This brings us to the matter of packaging and presentation. Research is essential, perhaps there is a favourite idea about the packaging, a family coat of arms, an image which is to be used. Think carefully about what the consumers expect, not what will please you, the producer. Your presentation should be consistent, select the message and image you want to get across to persuade consumers to buy and use your oil. Talk to consumers and distributors about what works and decide whether you are going with the norm or differentiate your product. If you have the resources, you may be able to engage a design consultant, if not, a graphic artist can help. You will need a label design, front and back, with images which can be used on your website.

There are specifications about the information which you must have on the labels, even as far as font size. The IOC international trade standards stipulate the words you can use, and food labelling requirements will guide you on the contents of the nutrition panel on the back label. The labelling regulations vary from country to country and should be researched before finalising the detail of the first label. The print run of the labels for your first production should consider that the label may need to be changed in the first few years as the product settles into the market and errors need correcting, or a new marketing angle is introduced.

Part of the story on our olive grove is the organic production and processing and wildlife which inhabits the grove – kangaroos, wallabies, echidnas and many species of birds. The farm is a wildlife sanctuary under the 'Land for Wildlife' initiative which promotes the conservation of fauna and flora on farms. To differentiate our product and to attract the attention of the conservation minded consumer we included the 'Land for Wildlife' logo on our front labels. We also included the organic certification which we dropped after ten years, so a new label run was required. Most certification organisations have regulations covering the use of the logo, the colour code and information permitted and require the label to be approved before use. They tend to introduce new regulations on labelling or new logos with little consideration for the cost of redesigning and printing labels. If there is a status or certification which is not assured and does not merit inclusion on the label, stickers can be used until the decision is made whether to continue with the approbation.

The paper used for the label should be carefully selected. Labels that stain when olive oil is spilled on them during pouring look soiled and unattractive. If the bottle leaks, even if sealed, the retailer cannot display it on the shelf. There is a range of label materials in the market and as it is the focal point of your product there should be no compromise on the quality of the label. If you are unsure of the suitability of the material offered, take some labels from the printer and test them with olive oil before making your decision.

The label must fit the bottle you select, or the tin if you are going to use them for larger volumes. The selection of the container is obviously pivotal in the presentation of your product. There are many websites offering all sizes of glass containers and tins with a range of qualities. Glass can be light run of the mill styles or heavy specially designed crystal. The weight of the glass packaging affects the weight of the packed cartons and may have an impact on freight and courier charges, something to be considered if selling online and using postal or courier delivery. The packaging you select should be determined by the market you are selling into, and any decision should be preceded by wide consultation with distributors, retailers and if foodservice, with chefs. Your own observation of the range of packaging on the shelf should give you an idea of the price range of oils in different packaging and the range of bottle styles. Beware of choosing tall bottles, they may look elegant and stylish, however they are unstable and easily knocked over, they do not fit into normal household store cupboards and are too tall for normal retail shelves as exemplified by supermarkets. Retail outlets will often have specifications on packaging which must be researched.

For the manufacturing quality of the bottle consult your packaging wholesaler as there are some substandard bottles offered directly from some countries and they do not have the strength necessary to withstand the handling along the supply chain. A carton of olive oil arriving with a broken bottle and oil everywhere is not a good advertisement for your product.

If tins are your choice of package, ensure that the manufacturing is food grade with the necessary linings and durability. Storage in some low quality tins for extended periods can lead to a distinctly cucumber aroma of the olive oil which may lead to it being deemed defective.

The closure you select will be dictated partly by regulation, and partly by choice. The European Union stipulates that extra virgin olive oil bottles have a non-refillable closure. The closures come in a range of options all of which have a plastic insert which acts as a non-drip pourer. Check the regulations and talk to bottlers about the most suitable closure which must be compatible with any machinery used for bottling and labelling. There are caps which can be applied manually for the small bottling runs for smaller producers. Some of these tend to leak, especially when airfreighted and can lead to rejection by the purchaser. Another problem with leaking caps is the leaked oil goes rancid very quickly and when opening a carton an unpleasant waft of rancidity greets the customer. The level to which a bottle is filled can also contribute to leakage. This occurs when the filling machine setting is incorrect and the quality control checking the filling level fails. This overfilling will also result in the loss of volume of oil.

Oxidisation of the olive oil while in the bottle must be limited as it leads to rancidity. For this reason, most extra virgin olive is packed in dark bottles. Some manufacturers pack olive oil in clear containers so the customer can see the colour of the oil. This packaging is mainly seen in the lower-priced high turnover supermarket brands.

There have been moves to ban packing olive oil in plastic containers in Spain. This edict would put refined olive oil and blended olive oil at a disadvantage with other vegetable oils mainly presented in the plastic containers which are much less costly than glass. One of the main reasons for this is apparently the environmental pollution with plastic worldwide. As one commentator observed, the problem is more one of inefficient recycling rather than the use of plastic. Notwithstanding this viewpoint, there are some questions about the suitability of plastic for olive oil relating to oxidisation and exposure to light and the health effects of phthalates which are used as plasticisers. These concerns may be contributing reasons for the ban on plastic which will pitch extra virgin olive oil and refined olive oil as an upmarket product when compared to vegetable oils. The ban extends to virtually all presentations of olive oil whatever the destination, including restaurants and other segments of the Horeca channel.

One relatively new entrant into the packaging market is the bag in the box presentation which is becoming more popular in foodservice where glass is a hazard. The container consists of a bladder made of metallised film contained in a cardboard box. The containers range from one litre up to larger sizes used for storing or transporting olive oil in bulk. One of the advantages of these containers is that the bladder collapses as oil is dispensed excluding air which, if present, leads to oxidisation in rigid containers unless the headspace is filled with nitrogen or another inert gas. The boxes of the bag in a box also exclude light unlike the plastic intermediate bulk containers (IBC) commonly used for storage and transport of olive oil.

The ideal container for bulk storage is a food grade stainless steel tank. These can range from five litres to thousands of litres. If combined with a system to fill the headspace with an inert gas as the olive oil is tapped off these stainless steel tanks, properly cleaned between fillings, will minimise oxidisation. Many boutique stores, especially the oil and vinegar stores in the USA, use small volume stainless steel fustis to dispense olive oil into bottles for customers on demand. This gives versatility for blending which is not offered if the oils are only offered in branded bottles. In some countries the refilling of bottles provided by customers is disallowed for some reason, in any instance the retailer should ensure the bottles proffered by customers are cleaned and have not been used for any other purpose or contained any other liquid.

Some large producers who supply into the Horeca channel have introduced a service whereby they deliver the olive oil in small stainless steel containers and replace them with fresh containers and oil when required. As part of the service the empty containers are collected, thoroughly cleaned and refilled ready for the next delivery. The arrangement saves the cost of disposable packaging, ensures the oil delivered is fresh, locks in the customer, and relieves the establishment of disposing of bulky containers. Perhaps an add-on to this service could be the removal of spent oil which in many countries cannot be disposed of in drains and must be retained for collection, refining and resale.

The decision on storage and packaging may result in a range of packaging for different markets and different products. The same can be said for the market segments you decide to use to sell your products; farmer's market, Horeca, boutique retail or supermarket.

Boutique Olive Oil Stores and Supermarkets

Some producers have opened boutique shops in shopping centres to sell their olive oil along with other olive-based products, olive oil soaps, table olives, olive wood artefacts, oil dispensers, and vinegars. Having visited these in many countries, Australia, New Zealand, South Africa, Spain, United Kingdom, France and USA, and talked to many participants in Savantes who run such outlets, the advice is to proceed with such an enterprise with caution. Location, location, location, is a saying in retail which resonates with olive oil.

Extra virgin olive oil is not a product which attracts customers like a wine shop or cellar, here the parallel with wine ends. Every shop I know which has sold only olive oil and olive products in Australia, New Zealand and South Africa has closed after a few years, unless there is another activity which attracts consumers. The successful ones have offered food, cheese or some other culinary attraction which draws the customers and olive oil becomes an add-on sale. There are of course exceptions such as the olive oil boutique in Sevilla near the cathedral which attracts the interest of tourists. The franchised Oil and Vinegar stores in the USA operate with varying degrees of success. One hears the publicity about the new openings but there is rarely publicity associated with stores which shut down. The successful stores are well located with innovative owners who offer a range of services and add-ons including tastings, food, kitchenware, vinegars and gift packs. One interesting activity is the stocking of the holiday homes of the well-heeled with food, including olive oil products, ready for their arrival in the holiday season!

From these boutique stores there is the whole range of retail outlets, organic groceries, grocery stores, restaurants for personalised packaging and, of course, supermarkets and hypermarkets. They range from the very personal boutiques with one-on-one contact with the customer through diminishing degrees of customer contact to the impersonal supermarkets where the only direct contact with the customer is an instore promotion. The very presence of boutiques in shopping malls is important in making potential customers aware of extra virgin olive oil and the activities of the owners in coaxing customers to try olive oil of different styles and flavours contributes to the growth of sales and consumption. This personal contact should be encouraged and innovative ways of bringing people into the stores developed and shared.

In some grocery stores seen in the USA there are two stations where olive oil is offered, the mainstream and less expensive brands are sold in the aisle along with vegetable oils and in the vegetable and fruit section a stand is set up with more upmarket extra virgin olive oils offered for sale and tasting. This seems ideal as there is a very suggestive association with food and cooking. In some stores there are the oils in the aisles and the upmarket extra virgin olive oils are on a shelf or in a cabinet in the delicatessen section. This does not seem as effective as the offering is more related to price differential than association with food.

The main aisle shelves where olive oil is offered with other vegetable oils are the domain of the big brands. Other than allowing a supermarket to carry a line of a locally produced olive oil, the buying and stocking of supermarkets is centralised with a category buyer. The buyer works in stock keeping units (sku) which are used to track inventory and stocks. The sku code contains information about each product such as supplier, brand, presentation and size. It is likely that the buyer will have responsibility for fulfilling a number of categories for a particular supermarket chain. The buying specifications are dictated throughout the chain and inclusion in the inventory is predicated more on the range, stock turnover and association with other products in the supermarket. For example a multi-national may supply a range of products, including olive oil, in many categories to one supermarket chain and has substantial influence to ensure its products are offered. Add to this the space on shelves is limited and usually up to five brands only are included. In countries which are new producers of olive oil the supermarkets may temporarily bow to the local pressure to include local products, however in a relatively short time the offering will fall back to five or less brands or sku's with one local brand now replacing a previous sku. The selection will be based on stock turnover and margins.

Many larger groceries and supermarkets have their own 'private label' olive oils of all classifications packaged specifically for them and competing with the branded products. The quality and price of these private label offerings are a direct challenge to the usually more expensive proprietary brands.

Access to supermarket shelves carries many compliance and contractual obligations. These include guarantees of supply and consistency of product with all the quality testing and maximum residue testing for pesticides and other chemical certifications. Delivery will be in specified amounts to a distribution centre. The supply contracts may include deductions for advertisement, promotion and other supermarket levies which will be taken off the agreed price before payment. There are penalties for inability to supply on time and massive penalties to cover product recall for non-compliance, including withdrawal costs from all outlets, centralisation, destruction of the product and payments for loss of trade. These penalties can run into hundreds of thousands of dollars, well beyond the means of small producers.

To meet the needs of the broad range of customers, many supermarkets require additional certification for kosher, halal and other guarantees covering the specific food statutes of religions. All these require expensive inspections and certification fees by the appointed representatives of the specific religious group, usually on an annual basis.

To fully understand the costs of supply to a supermarket there are spreadsheets available where the costs associated with each input, stage of supply and imposts are separately identified and can be varied according to the requirements of each buyer. Supermarkets conduct annual or more frequent reviews of their product lines where suppliers are invited to submit their prices for continued supply.

If one brand dominates the olive oil shelves and starts to exercise its power as a sole supplier, the supermarket chain may invite another supplier to introduce a brand which competes and gives the supermarket more flexibility in its negotiations. Private label lines are sometimes introduced to achieve the same end.

These are the options a producer has when deciding how to sell the first harvest. The channel will depend largely on the size of the enterprise and yield in the first year. The initial market entry must consider the expected eventual yield when the grove reaches full production. Very often, the independence of smaller volume producers tends to lead them to undertake the marketing and sales in their own right. There are examples in the main producing regions where this is prevalent such as Italy and Greece, whereas Spanish small producers tend to aggregate into cooperatives. There are successful enterprises adopting the different associations to present their product to consumers and the dynamics are constantly changing to meet the perceived needs of producers and consumers. Recently in Crete several producer associations combined to market olive oil products from the Greek island in a cohesive way while some producers who have successfully sold their own extra virgin olive oil will continue to do so independently.

The seasons in some years result in the production of a style of olive oil which varies from the norm and challenges the producer to continue the consistency of their product. The options are to retain some oil from the previous year and use this to moderate the flavour profile of the oil or to seek a partner producer who can exchange oils of the required profile. This short-term solution to balance the flavour profile of the new season oils may lead to longer term arrangements which are strategically convenient to explore new markets such as exports.

Exporting

Exporting extra virgin olive oils and being able to brag about them being on the shelves of famous stores such as Trader Joe's in the USA, Fortnum and Mason or Sainsbury's in the UK and similar stores in Europe can boost sales at home. Exporting is complex, requiring a plethora of export and import licences, tariffs, compliance from the processing facility right through to delivery to the retailer, adherence to trade standards and meeting the labelling and other requirements in the importing country. The time taken from leaving the producer's facilities to arriving in the consumer's hands in another country necessitates more attention to degradation and shelf-life than local sales. There are risks of having containers held-up from strikes, political action on imports, off-the-shelf testing in the destination country aimed at discrediting imports, slow payment, plagiarising the brand and filling the bottle with substitute oil and loss of containers and damage caused by mishandling. Insurance against all these potential mishaps is essential.

The message is to proceed into export markets with extreme caution, get to know the system and its nuances and engage with others who can help with the potential problems in the destination country. In Asian countries especially, it is wise, if not essential, to establish a partnership or similar relationship with a business in the countries to which the product is being exported.

Small volume producers may find that the cost of freighting their product to the importing country precludes exporting independently. There are options to work with an importer, such as an online retailer, who can aggregate small batches of products in the source country to fill a container. Producers can cooperate to achieve this as well, perhaps working through an association or establishing an export cooperative.

Quality

The next essential competitive advantage is the quality of the olive oil product. Quality is possibly the most used and misused word in the global olive oil industry. It means something different to every person who uses it, producer, consumer, trader, bureaucrat, scientist, and marketer. This ambiguity is accommodated in the dictionary definitions, the ultimate reference, the simplest among many being 'of high standard'. This means that any olive oil product can be described as quality, be it refined, blended or extra virgin. Anyone who has worked in the olive oil refining industry and tasted a range of refined olive oils will realise that there are low quality and high quality refined oils, all, to be pedantic, are quality in their specified category.

The producers and marketers of extra virgin olive oils seem to have highjacked the term 'quality' to be applied exclusively to their products. Their definition of high and low quality extra virgin olive oil is predicated on the free fatty acidity and polyphenol level, or intensity of the oil. The consequence of this is that consumers are regaled with the word quality which, because of its overuse and multiple connotations, has been devalued. The definition of a quality olive oil is driven by technicians on classification panels, researchers, administrators, politicians and marketers.

The very classification system introduced to ensure that all olive oil made available for human consumption is of a high standard, or quality, is in place to ensure that consumers receive quality olive oil. The undermining of this classification by vested interests subverting the term quality to suit their purposes is a problem for the industry as it confuses consumers. This is especially confusing for them when the purveyors of the top 5% of extra virgin olive oil claim that only their olive oil is quality, thereby denigrating the other 95% of classified olive oil as inferior, despite it being of superior quality to competing vegetable oils. Perpetuating this divisiveness does the entire industry a disservice.

Value for Money

To introduce a reference which may have greater resonance with consumers, Savantes teamed up with The North American Olive Oil Association (NAOOA) to test the introduction of a 'value for money' codification for olive oils. For an annual Olive Oil Conference held in Chicago a set of olive oils and blends were purchased from a grocery chain and sent to Spain for testing of the fatty acid profiles and smoke point. The set comprised a high priced extra virgin olive oil, a medium priced extra virgin olive oil, a refined olive oil, a blend of refined olive oil and extra virgin olive oil, and a blend of canola oil and extra virgin olive oil. The oils were then allocated points for flavour, smoke point and fatty acid profile. For smoke point the score was 1-5 with five being awarded to the highest range of smoke point of 226°C to 235°C to one for the lowest range from 180°C to 190°C. For the fatty acid profile score, an oil with below 60% monounsaturated fatty acids received one point to oils with 76% and above receiving five points. As would be expected the refined oil and blends received the highest scores of three and four for smoke point with the extra virgin olive oils attaining a score of two for the range of 191-200 °C. The scores for monounsaturated fatty acids were three for the canola oil blended with extra virgin olive oil, four for the refined olive oil blends and five for the two extra virgin olive oils. For the flavour profile the extra virgin olive oils were given a notional score of 25 out of 25, the extra virgin olive oil blends with refined olive oil a score of 10 and the refined olive oil with no flavour scored 0.

The polyphenol count was not scored separately as this was considered part of the flavour profile and did not warrant additional scores. The scores for the five oils were totalled with a possible perfect score of 35. The highest scoring olive oils on this basis were the two extra virgin olive oils on 32 points. Of course, I can hear the readers saying, they are the highest qualities so that makes sense. The high score is attributable to the notional 25 points given for flavour. However, when the score was divided by the shelf-price of cost per ounce to give value for money, the picture changed with the medium priced extra virgin olive oil scoring the highest with 45.07, then came the canola/extra virgin olive oil blend at 39.53, the refined olive oil came in at 32, the olive oil or refined extra virgin olive oil blend scored 31.48 and the high price extra virgin olive oil came last with a value score of 23.02. All the oils were bought at the same store with the canola-extra virgin olive oil blend being blended from the high price extra virgin olive oil and purchased canola oil, the price adjusted pro rata. The influence of the variability of prices between retail outlets was therefore eliminated.

There will be many arguments about the weighting of flavour and the notional flavour scores, the exclusion of a score for the polyphenol level and the relative weightings given to the monounsaturated fatty acid percentage and smoke point. The polyphenol levels of the oils were measured with the range being the high price Italian extra virgin olive oil being 252mg/kg, the medium price Greek extra virgin olive oil 204mg/kg, the olive oil blend 84mg/kg, the canola oil blend 78mg/kg and the refined olive oil less than 17mg/kg. Those offering the arguments will most likely come from the vested interest of seeing their product scoring well in the value score.

We were surprised by the result having gone into the exercise fully expecting the extra virgin olive oils to outscore all the blends and refined olive oil. Before presenting these results to the conference participants we decided to make the factual data of smoke point, monounsaturated fat and price available to them. By providing the five oils for them to taste blind and give their own score for flavour out of 25, they could calculate their personal value for money score. The result of this exercise was even more surprising given that the participants were mostly professionals from the olive oil industry with the selling and evaluation of olive oil being part of their daily activity. Generally, they reduced the flavour score differential between the extra virgin olive oils and the blends, in some cases lifting the value for money score of the blends higher than that for the extra virgin olive oils.

The discussion was animated with many disconcerted by this challenge to the mantra of robust extra virgin olive oil being the highest quality and the most desirable. The exercise was edifying and serves to expose the gap between the conventional wisdom of the sellers as to what is the best value and the real value given the flavour and physical benefits for the consumer. The consensus at the Olive Oil Conference hosted in Chicago by the NAOOA and Savantes in 2016 was that the first comprehensive presentation of the 'Value for Money' concept revealed some surprising insights. The main conclusion from the ensuing discussion was that the system needed to be simplified if there was to be any chance of it being used as a marketing tool.

This idea was first presented by me at the inaugural QvExtra! Conference in Cordoba, Spain in 2013 during a session on the meaning of quality. The proposition was that the most important criterion for the consumer was value for money, a function of quality and price. The idea was not warmly received by a traditional audience to which it was a new concept and comprised of producers of generally high polyphenol, robust and high priced extra virgin olive oil which may not fare well on the value for money scale.

It is unlikely that the idea will be adopted by associations or representative organisations because of the potential to disadvantage some members who will have a multitude of opinions as to the importance and loading of each of the criteria used to calculate the value. While the smoke point and monounsaturated fatty acid levels are arrived at through independent analysis the flavour profile, assessment is subjective, and the price will vary between retail channels. Notwithstanding the resistance and obstacles in establishing a simple and coherent formula, the opportunity is there for some brand or group to adopt the approach and establish a credible market advantage for their product. Unfortunately, disagreement on detail often leads to inertia.

Flexibility

Flexibility is a competitive advantage in being able to meet the changing needs of the olive oil market. It can be built into a business from the initial decisions on location, production unit size, varieties planted, grove management and market segments targeted. An example is the ability to switch from olive oil to table olive production if the price differential is conducive to making the change. This can only be done if the production base has dual purpose varieties, and the layout accommodates harvesting for table olives.

Planting a range of varietals in the same or different groves gives the flexibility of extended pollination, different harvesting times, and disease and insect resistance. Having groves in different locations reduces the risk of local weather events causing damage to the entire production source, and recently there is the flexible option of getting supply from the northern or southern hemisphere bringing fresh oil into blends or as varietal lines twice a year.

Having the capacity to store the different varietal oils separately gives great flexibility in blending consistent products as the different oils oxidise at different rates. An example of lack of flexibility is the inability of a Greek producer to store a differentiated oil from a variety other than koroneiki separately to give another product line commanding a higher price.

Being able to adjust to market trends which provide the opportunity to blend with other vegetable oils such as avocado oil will enhance market presence through increased competitive advantage over inflexible suppliers.

Flexibility in pricing brings us to the critical determinant of sales – price. An edifying experience occurred at an olive oil mill in Cordoba many years ago when an olive oil consultant from Sevilla demonstrated the art of blending. Having an array of olive oils from different campaigns, with delicate to robust flavour profiles and different bulk prices, he asked which market, flavour profile and wholesale price the buyer would like. With his spreadsheet of the chemical profiles of the oils he proceeded to blend the oil requested with the shelf-life needed for the market channel, the required flavour profile at the right price. This was a demonstration of professional expertise providing great flexibility for the producer to supply the buyer with the product requested. A far cry from the approach of many smaller producers which is to produce a product and sell it into the market as a function of production and not demand.

Pricing

Price is the single most important inducement for a consumer to purchase a product. Ultimately the consumer sets the price for a commodity, if the price is unacceptable, consumers will buy another product.

Pricing is complex with every stage of the supply chain adding costs and profit as the product passes through their hands. For an industry to function efficiently each stage should be profitable, if there are too many stages and profit margins become too small, stages will be cut out or bypassed. The market can be segmented into four general tiers which are the same as any other industry. At the top end there are the high priced boutique products which offer something new and innovative, something luxurious which gives the buyer a feeling of largesse, affluence or authority. The next tier covers the high-end products which offer higher quality than the mainstream products and are differentiated in many ways – origin, flavour, health attributes, marketing, packaging, organic production, bird safe and many more.

These two higher priced categories make up approximately 10% of the olive oil market globally, with some variation between countries. The olive oil offered is exclusively extra virgin olive oil with a range of certifications guaranteeing quality. We can call this end of the market the 'high-end' with relatively low volume and high value.

The next tier is by far the largest by volume and total value and includes hypermarkets, supermarkets, groceries and other food stores. High turnover of lower priced brands of all classifications and blends of olive oil are on offer to consumers in a range of glass, plastic and tin containers from 500ml to four litres. Included in this segment of high turnover and low margins is the Horeca channel covering food service.

The final tier is where olive oils are discounted at low prices to clear stocks, attract customers to stores as loss leaders and to sell products close to the best before dates.

Special offers can be included in this category, however as a common marketing strategy, offering special deals on olive oil is used throughout all the market segments.

Online sales which received a boost during the pandemic lockdowns cross all channels from boutique to supermarket and Horeca.

The consumer decides on price early in the shopping experience. With the range of vegetable oils offered the first decision is whether to use olive oil in preference to other oils. The next decision is whether to use it for all cooking or just as a raw oil for salads or selective inclusion as an ingredient. These decisions are made because of ethnic or family tradition, exposure to positive marketing messages, knowledge of the benefits of the various vegetable oils, perceived value for money and disposable income. There is a degree of fickleness at the lower priced end of the olive oil products with consumers switching between olive oil and vegetable oils on a regular basis predicated on affordability and special offers. Generally, this group purchases the cheaper refined olive oils with low flavour profiles like the vegetable oils they are used to. There is more stability in the sales of the extra virgin olive oil grade of olive oil where the more committed users of olive oil show their willingness to spend more on a product which has both health and culinary benefits.

These buying patterns give the industry multiple opportunities to increase the volume and value of olive oil sales. First to attract buyers who use vegetable oils or animal fats and induce them to use olive oil when they can afford it or when convinced it has utility and benefits in their home cooking. Then to move these consumers from occasional use to regular use, then exclusive use of olive oil. The next, and sometimes concurrent, steps are to persuade the users of refined olive oils to use extra virgin olive oils, then higher quality extra virgin olive oils, and then to increase the volume used in each household. This progressive conversion and careful targeting of each group of potential and existing users of olive oil should increase consumption more than efforts to convert non-users directly to robust flavour extra virgin olive oil.

The marketing predisposes consumers to purchase olive oil prior to their decision as to where to shop. The shopping destination will predetermine the quality and price of the olive oil available to the shopper. The greater volumes will be sold through supermarkets with the smaller volumes sold at a substantially higher price in specialty olive oil stores which are a destination for the most committed olive oil users.

In the same way, the producers commit themselves to selling their oil in a particular price range when deciding on the retail outlets where their product will be offered. Following the initial smaller harvests, the producer can build their sales strategies to access markets with greater throughput and returns on their investment. It is more astute to build into these markets than to enter a market initially where the supply and price cannot be sustained.

One market entry strategy is to develop two or three styles of extra virgin olive oil from a delicate flavour profile through medium to a robust oil. When presenting your product this gives you other options if the buyer does not like the initial offering. Pricing can be correlated to the intensity and the need to move the more delicate product with lower polyphenols and shorter shelf-life faster than the medium and robust oils. This would suggest a lower price for the delicate oil initially. If the higher priced robust oil does not move as rapidly as hoped, it has longer shelf-life allowing more time to sell it, and it can be blended with the delicate oil to give a middle priced medium intensity oil.

As the yield from the grove increases the olive oils can be aligned with your range of products already in the marketplace and to some extent harvesting can be adjusted to boost the volume of the best seller. Having multiple brands and prices is a tactic used by large producers to sell oil in each segment: boutique, high-end and mainstream supermarket.

As mentioned previously, one often hears of the need to educate consumers about the virtues of extra virgin olive oil and olive oil in general. This call to improve the knowledge about olive oil products comes from many sectors and levels in the industry. Occasions where the knowledge of the vendors, those who should impart the knowledge, have been tested with simple tasting tests shows that the knowledge of flavour profiles, varieties and defects is generally less than satisfactory. It seems the industry would get better returns by educating or training salespeople and managers so that the communication with consumers is pitched at the right level.

Quality Control

Product knowledge in the supply chain will potentially reduce the delivery of sub-standard product when buyers and salespeople can taste and detect defects and refuse to sell the oil. Currently the common approach is to have a quality control department staffed by technicians who have responsibility for ensuring the olive oil being sold meets trade standards and is free of defects. The tendency is therefore to leave all quality control to this department and the salespeople take little interest or responsibility in the quality of the product they are given to sell. An appropriate anecdote here is that of a highly successful homewares store in Australia which considered its shop salespeople the most important of its employees. They argued that the whole business depended on the transactions completed across the counter instore. The family-owned company invested substantially in the training of their staff with product knowledge being central to the curriculum. The store staff had direct input into buying policy and buyers responded directly to the requirements of the customers as assessed by the stores. To reinforce the philosophy, the company administration was called Support Group and not Head Office or Headquarters. The owners received persistent requests to establish a 'Customer Complaints' department to deal with the daily complaints coming from over 120 stores in three countries. They steadfastly refused, stating that customer satisfaction was every employee's responsibility, and every staff member had the power to deal with complaints as they saw fit. By decentralising the responsibility for complaints to stores they saved themselves the cost of another department, sorted the complaints out very quickly at source and the staff dealing with them instore applied pressure back on the buyers and administration to sort out their systems or product purchasing.

This model would serve the olive oil industry well with salespeople rejecting faulty product and being able to respond to consumers' requirements in a timely way. The rejection of sub-standard product, or one with an inappropriate flavour profile, by one's own salesforce would put pressure back on the downstream suppliers to improve their knowledge and quality control. A simple test of the effectiveness and return on investment of training to improve product knowledge would be to give the salespeople in one region advanced training and monitor whether the results are better than those from relatively untrained staff in similar regions. Having staff with excellent product knowledge would put pressure on those at management level to have at least equal, or better, product knowledge. Put bluntly, before the olive oil industry admonishes consumers for lack of knowledge, the industry itself needs to enhance its product knowledge throughout and increase its investment in training of its salesforce. The training should be sales oriented with the technical component a means to an end and not the end itself.

My experience is that the product knowledge in the producing countries is reasonable, however in the trade in the main importing countries such as the USA it is well below par. Much is invested by the producing countries in increasing the knowledge of consumers in importing countries, it seems little is invested in training the participants in the distribution system.

Flowing on from enhanced training will be the ability to provide continuing support and training to retailers and consumers. After-sales service is an important component of any transaction. This is exemplified by a large progressive company involved in olive oil in the USA which invited all its major buyers from foodservice to attend a taste training programme in New York. The apparent philosophy behind the initiative was to give their clients the capacity to distinguish between the high quality products the company offered and those offered to them by other suppliers. The confidence in their own products was shown by the independence of the presentations and olive oils offered for tasting which did not include the company's products. An additional achievement was to get the sales executives from competing foodservice suppliers in the one room for a few days and set aside differences to concentrate on their olive oil products. The investment in having more discerning clients across the whole industry would lift both the quality of service and product.

Downstream monitoring of olive oil products is important as they oxidise and, depending on the storage and packaging, will become rancid. This is a problem at retail level with slow moving stock sitting on shelves under lights for extended periods. While it is the responsibility of the retailer to control and monitor the quality of olive oil stocks, ultimately it is the brand which suffers through customer complaints and negative reports in consumer magazines or compliance testing. This reinforces the importance of training retailers to monitor stock and controlling supply to those stores with slow moving lines to minimise the risk of rancidity. Simple practices such as putting the replacement stock behind the unsold stock when restacking shelves and informing managers when stock with new best before dates is supplied will reduce the chances of oil going rancid on shelves. A useful practice is for the salesperson to purchase a bottle off the shelf from stores and check the quality. In smaller boutique retailers with slow moving stock, it may be beneficial to offer to replace product past its best before date or encourage the retailer to put it on sale at least two months before expiry with the promise of fresh stocks from the new season.

Product knowledge is essential for effective promotion. There are the industry-wide promotions at national and international level over which individual producers have little or no control. To fund these, levies are often collected by government or other institutions and allocated to marketers to deliver awareness campaigns directed at influencers or consumers.

Individuals then take advantage of these promotional efforts by adding their own advertising and promotional activities to the extent the budget will allow. These are activities over which the producer or distributor exercises a large degree of control.

You Are Always Marketing

You are always marketing. Everything you do in relation to your product will be judged by those you are seeking to impress and persuade to buy your product. The way you dress, your timeliness, efficiency in following up on meetings and orders, speed of responding to queries, your knowledge and every facet of your business activities have an impression on your customer. If you are selling at a farmer's market, for authenticity, dress and behave like a farmer. If possible, research the customary dress of the businesses you are meeting with to present your products. It is not just the quality of the olive oil in the bottle you are selling, it is the whole package of product, service, professionalism and efficiency. Check which language the buyer prefers and try to use the vernacular and vocabulary of the segment of the industry you are selling into to show you understand the market. Do not assume the person you are dealing with is bereft of knowledge, by way of conversation explore their ability to taste, their preferences and bias, and their depth of knowledge. Pitch your presentation giving them credit for the knowledge they have, treat them with respect.

Many businesses have a uniform embellished with the brand logo and slogan. This adds professionalism in some instances and is inappropriate in some environments, especially those at senior management level where more formal business attire is expected. Promotional caps, aprons and other branded products are often given as gifts, most end up in cupboards never to be used. Some people will not wear clothing which can be seen as free advertising or competing with their own brand. If you are going to give gifts, give something useful and different.

Within reason, when you leave a meeting, those who you leave behind should have something different to remember you by, it may be some data, information, a differentiated product or a gift. Most buyers, chefs, retailers get approached by many producers or distributors on a weekly or daily basis, offering similar products at similar prices with similar sales pitches. Be different, differentiate your approach as much as you differentiate your product.

Beyond ascertaining the level of product knowledge of your potential customer, research, without being intrusive, their hobbies or personal interests so you can develop a conversation with them which builds more than just the sales relationship. This is not a suggestion that inducements are used as many are wary of receiving these lest it be seen as corruption, however, like all industries, they are offered by some to receive favourable consideration. An example is paid visits to a producer's groves for journalists with the expectation that favourable articles are written in selected newspapers.

Promotion starts at the local level by spreading information about the excellence of the operation through employees, politicians, vendors and local administration. It is not only the dealings with potential buyers which builds brand recognition and respect.

Based at the home locality are also the promotions on the internet and social media. On all platforms your message and brand presentation should be consistent, memorable and repeatable. The language should be uncomplicated and recognise the interests of your consumers. Fundamentally, the use of olive oil is a food ingredient and while the family, your grove, processing and packaging may be very important to you, it is less important to customers. They need to be assured of flavour for the use in food at an affordable price. They want consistency and value for money. The images and persuasive language on your internet communication should be of food and its enjoyment, its social significance and the well-being it generates. Use pictures of families eating together, ordinary people cooking in home kitchens, not celebrities cooking in studio kitchens. Relate the stories to customers.

Using the Internet

Most websites promoting olive oil, be they multi-national brands or boutique estate brands have one website to fit all. There are options for translation to different languages, mainly European, and the option to use online translations. The images and narrative do not change when selecting a different language despite the ethnicity and cuisine of the searching entity probably being different from the source of the olive oil. Smart marketing would be to have the images change to represent the consumers of the destination country, the pictures of food changing to their cuisine and where appropriate, the narrative or promotional text adjusting to pitch messages suitable for their culture. The products and packaging would represent those available in the relevant countries. This approach would take a different mindset from that of selling the Mediterranean diet and using flavour descriptors which pertain to the foods from the Mediterranean countries, the one message fits all promotion. The development exercise would require some research into the preferences and foods of the different countries which will be beneficial to the producers in getting into the minds of the consumers.

Social media platforms such as Facebook, Instagram, Twitter, YouTube, WhatsApp, Messenger, WeChat, QQ, Qzone, Tik Tok, and Linkedin are another vehicle used by many olive oil brands to promote their products and connect with consumers. This provides a very direct line to consumers with specific platforms being popular with different market segments and countries, for example QQ and Tik Tok are popular amongst Chinese consumers. Individuals can upload blogs, videos and comments promoting their products with advertising available on most of these sites. Care should be taken to avoid personal posts promoting goods and services, such as olive oil tasting schools and brands, being uploaded on personal sites where personal political commentary on unrelated issues is likely to offend some followers.

Promotional Activities

Other promotional activities beyond the local area are regional, national and international conferences and events which offer sponsorships. The return to the sponsor may be in the form of use of their olive oil in food being provided to participants, cooking demonstrations, inclusion in promotional material and conference proceedings, opportunities to present papers and inclusion of product in conference satchels. As these events generally involve industry participants, the promotion is more towards the supply chain operators than consumers. However, fringe benefits may be press and media coverage which exposes the brand to a much wider audience and consumers.

Product placement is emerging as an effective form of promotion in the visual arts, mainly film-making for cinema and television. Cooking shows and reality culinary series like MasterChef and My Kitchen Rules on television. and online videos, are obvious places for exposure of olive oil brands for use in cooking.

Lifestyle, travel and cooking books and magazines are still in demand despite the prevalence of digital media. Books have been written about olive groves, olive oil tasting naming particular brands, food regions and associated olive oil flavours. Cooking books are as popular as ever and while some advocate the use of generic olive oil as a cooking medium or ingredient, others name brands and describe the flavour profiles. Online blogs and newsletters offer the same opportunities for brand promotion.

At national and international level for larger producers and corporations there are trade shows in every importing country. The target audience varies from olive oil industry traders, food distributors and consumers. Visitors to some shows are limited to traders with the general consumer excluded. Exhibiting at the shows is sometimes organised by country trade commissions to reduce the costs of space and there may be some subsidies to cover other costs. Travel and accommodation, exhibitor stand rental, equipment and services and other costs make participation as an exhibitor expensive and beyond the reach of many small producers. The events provide an opportunity to contact potential buyers and establish leads, as well as meeting existing buyers and showing a presence. Selection of the trade shows in which to participate should be preceded by careful consideration of the target market, assessment of the attendance at previous similar events and, if possible, discussion with those who have exhibited in the past.

For smaller producers, access to these events is achieved by participating in an exhibit which aggregates several products into one stand. The proponent may be an importer or an online sales platform who exhibits its range of products and invites the salespeople from each producer to attend and assist during the show. This assists the vendor and provides the producer with a cost-effective sales opportunity.

Those travelling from other countries to trade shows may take the opportunity to visit retailers who stock their product to participate in instore promotion. This is a popular low cost way of assisting the retailer, exposing products and communicating with consumers.

Health Benefits of Olive Oil

The health benefits of extra virgin olive oil dominate the promotion of olive oil products across the world. Hardly a day passes without a media release from a research institution or publicity campaign claiming or proclaiming the health benefits of olive oil, especially as a part of the Mediterranean diet. The information contained can be divided into three categories: indicative, part proven and proven. Olive oil is a food and can be expected to have beneficial effects on human metabolism in providing a range of nutrients required for cell structure and maintenance, energy and general functioning of the human organs. Extra virgin olive oil has the added benefits of the polyphenols which act as antioxidants limiting the formation and destructive activity of free radicals. It must be noted that many of the compounds found in extra virgin olive oil are found in other foods, especially vegetables, which contain high levels of antioxidants. The levels of polyphenols in a range of food ingredients ranks olive oil 61st when measured as mg/100g, and estimates undertaken by Savantes and presented during programmes indicates the cost per serve of polyphenols obtained from extra virgin olive oils is approximately AU$0.26, ranking below everyday foods such as green olives, broccoli and almonds.

Notwithstanding this data which shows that extra virgin olive oil is one of many sources of nutrients and antioxidants, it contains in one product the healthy nutrients which would need to be sourced from many ingredients. It also has synergistic affects with other food ingredients such as tomatoes with the antioxidant lycopene, the red carotenoid pigment giving the tomato its colour.

Some of the health-giving actions of olive oil are indicative, in other words initial research has shown there may be beneficial effects and more research is needed. Among the diseases for which benefits have been identified are cardiovascular disease, diabetes, breast cancer, colon cancer, inflammation, and osteoporosis. Careful examination of the publicity and announcements relating to the health benefits of olive oil reveals many are generated by research institutions seeking funding to continue research and maintain research capability, courtesy of funding provided by the industry. The research covers disease prevention and population analysis, often related to the benefits of the Mediterranean diet funded by the olive oil and health industries. There are substantial books available to clinicians dedicated to the health and medical benefits of consuming olive oil. The benefit to the sales of olive oil is the ability to publicise these benefits on the labels and in promotional material. The right to include health claims is regulated in many countries with only the substantiated benefits being allowed with many disallowed for not being substantiated, only indicative. There is much continuing research to substantiate the indicative benefits and have them included in the regulators list of allowable claims.

Some brands have circumvented the rules relating to claims of health benefits which can be included on labels by including website addresses where the health claims are listed. Recently in Spain this practice has been curtailed.

From a producer's perspective one must question how much evidence is enough to establish the olive oil product as the healthiest vegetable oil and whether some of the continuing investment in clinical research would be better spent in creating awareness of existing research results amongst consumers leading to increased consumption. The pot of money for health research is attractive to researchers in public health institutions to expand their research portfolio and encourages new 'olive oil' research initiatives from newcomer universities outside the main producing countries, arguably to expand their research capability. In many cases it appears that the research projects are repeating completed research or are running concurrent research projects with the same aims. To avoid this waste of research funding the IOC should have a register of all research being undertaken by institutions and agencies worldwide as a reference for funding agencies when assessing the value of research proposals. The IOC facility could be funded by the savings from duplication of research with money over to invest in the implementation of research results through promoting directly the increased consumption of olive oil globally. The rationalisation of research would facilitate a shift in promotion from domination of health benefits to more pragmatic and tangible benefits to the consumer such as flavour and use in cooking in the homes of the people in countries worldwide.

One of the consequences of the multitude of claims of the health benefits of olive oil is the attempt by competing vegetable oils to engineer their product to mirror olive oil, especially the monounsaturated fat component. Cold pressing of other seed oils and use of the descriptor extra virgin also attracts the consumer at the expense of the pioneering extra virgin olive oil. This development reinforces the need to promote extra virgin olive as a complete food ingredient with flavour and concomitant health benefits.

Keeping the Source Happy

'Keep your trees happy' should be the maxim of olive grove managers. They are living with a time-honoured ability to survive almost anything short of catastrophic by adjusting their metabolism and reproductive mode.

Management through the year involves the repetitive cycle of harvesting, pruning, suckering, flowering, and fruit-set, all supported by the intervention of water application, weed, pest and disease control.

Modern practice of super high-density groves with mechanical pruning and harvesting is designed to reduce costs and either increase profit margins at current prices or reduce the ultimate retail price for consumers to increase consumption and therefore expand the market. The horticultural practices are being driven by human needs of profit and are not necessarily in the best horticultural interests of the tree.

Producers now use drones to assist in fruit counts to estimate yield, fruit ripening and loosening chemicals are applied to control ripening and harvest timing, computerised irrigation systems and other techniques are installed to maximise production and oil yield and minimise the cost of labour.

This modernity has social implications for producing countries which are shifting the management of groves from small farmers to broadacre corporate operations with highly trained technicians operating harvesting and pruning equipment and computerised oil extraction mills. Change in the global olive oil industry is accelerating with increased production and prosperity predicated on the advent of the super high-density groves stalled by the decline in consumption in producing countries and the lack of increase in global consumption.

An oversupply of olive oil will bring prices down and temporarily increase consumption. The resulting lack of profitability for small and medium size producers will force many out of the industry with those remaining severely curtailing their spending. This reduced spending will in turn cause social disruption in towns which depend on the olive oil industry for their prosperity.

Climate events such as drought will have the opposite effect of decreasing production with consequential increases in price of olive oil. This will also squeeze the producer's margin as costs are spread over a smaller volume of product.

Looking for Leadership

The situation requires leadership at all levels. Leadership from within the olive oil industry, not from external political or academic institutions where the interests are not necessarily compatible with or complimentary to the global olive oil industry. The industry shows the classic tensions between liberty and equality, community and efficiency explored in James O'Toole's 'The Executive's Compass - Business and the Good Society'. O'Toole held many senior positions in leadership forums in the USA, including the highly respected 'Aspen Institute Executive Seminar' where leaders are brought together to be exposed to classic literature and discussion of the role values play in society.

The tension between liberty and equality can be summed up as the difference between a society where one is free to pursue one's own interests in an environment of uncontrolled supply and demand, and a society where centralised control is used to moderate disparities in wealth and power. An example in the olive industry would be the difference between a country which has no subsidies or import tariffs on olive oil, and one where producers are subsidised, and tariffs applied on imports.

The tension between community and efficiency is the difference between global competition using technology to drive down production costs and deliver cheaper products, and the maintenance of quality of life which flows from traditional methods. In the olive industry this tension is well demonstrated by the difference between the traditional small olive groves in the Mediterranean countries and the super high-density, mechanically harvested, groves which are being developed mainly in Spain and Portugal. At stake is the destruction of the family-based traditional farms and the dominance of the corporately owned new groves.

Currently a notional 'Olive Industry Compass' is weighted towards liberty and efficiency giving the corporations and venture capitalists a distinct advantage in influence in the industry and political decisions. This is a substantial shift from the lobbying strength of the farmer cooperatives in Europe dating back to the emergence of the economies from the combative early half of the twentieth century.

Agrarian influence from regions where agriculture dominates is often courted by politicians who tend to deliver benefits to their electors and ignore the need to apply pressure for the advancement of capabilities. The result is a widening gap between the small producer, relatively unworldly, who delivers olives for processing, and the cooperative or corporation on which he or she relies to provide knowledge and support. An example of the apparent exploitation of producers is the recent enactment of laws in Spain requiring processors or traders to pay farmers within 30 days of delivery of their oil or olives. This suggests that the producers have been powerless to force the timely payment for their work and the processors will exploit arrangements for their own financial gain, perpetuating the dependency on them. Another example of centralised control is the notion that in Greece it is better to 'work with government' with bureaucracy blunting innovation and frustrating young progressive producers. This needs to change to a weighting which delivers more equality and nurtures the community.

This does not suggest the elimination of the current emphasis of entrepreneurial freedom and business efficiency, rather it suggests that this should be the generator which drives the equality and community development agenda. Much of the narrative used by conglomerates to market extra virgin olive oil is based on the union between cultures and food in the Mediterranean countries, the centrality of the olive groves to community and social and physical well-being. The souls of the olive oil industry.

Through large scale commercialisation and mechanisation extra virgin will become a commodity with no more soul than the broad acres of seed oil crops with massive tractors pulling tilling equipment and sowing genetically engineered seed to be harvested by banks of massive combine harvesters. Soulless mass production which exploits the environment, uses vast quantities of inorganic fertilisers, pesticides, herbicides and other chemicals used to solvent extract the oils. A soulless commoditised olive oil industry will dismantle the communal fabric of regional Spain, Italy, Greece and to a lesser extent other Mediterranean, Aegean and Adriatic countries.

It is the responsibility of the industry to recognise the destructive forces of unbridled industrialisation and design a future which develops leading edge technology and at the same time nurtures the traditional production from which the industry has grown and the small producers, those 'ordinary' people, whose resilience has seen them survive economic and social revolutions over centuries.

If we apply the compass to the olive industry it will use the production of extra virgin olive oil and the performance of corporate and high-density mechanised production to nurture traditional and cooperative production in the regions. The Spanish Government has flagged a proposal to identify the production from small producers in the marketplace to encourage consumers to support them. This already happens through differentiation of price and has not halted the pressure on small producers. Governments collect taxes and redistribute the money to support industries and projects which are aligned with their policies. Sometimes this benefits smaller olive oil producers through subsidies, sometimes it is channelled elsewhere.

As the numbers and political influence of the traditional producers diminish, the support will subside proportionately. It is time the producers took matters into their own hands and adopted a strategy of training and professionalisation which equips them with the capacity to define their own destiny. A suggestion to an olive oil mill in Spain that their staff be trained and empowered to manage sections of the processing and distribution, responding to complaints and innovating in their own right was rejected out of hand by one of the owners who said such a managerial arrangement was not possible in Spain, implying that the employees did not want the responsibility or the capability.

This is convenient to retain the status quo; it means the status quo will be maintained throughout the industry and it will be left behind as competitors progress and continue to sequester more of the vegetable oil market. The olive oil industry is captive of its own inertia, believing that extra virgin olive oil will change the world and not the people who produce and use it.

Time for Change

It is time for change, change which rarely comes from the incumbent administration at all levels whose tenure is transient and not grounded in the environment of the 'ordinary people'. The industry hierarchy, including the IOC, are not achieving their primary aim of improving the well-being of the ordinary people who derive their income from olive oil because their administration and enactment of rules has become an end in itself and not a means to increase consumption of olive oil. It is time for a peaceful revolution starting in the dispersed regions where producers are concentrated.

The first stage is self-advancement leading to greater dexterity in representing their interests and wresting control from those who now derive their income and power from all the services growing around the supply chain, sapping the lifeblood of olive oil producers and using it to fuel their own research, bureaucratic and political interests. The second stage is to reduce the dependency on the extended supply chain and bring the interests of consumers closer to the producers, shedding layers of regulation and compliance which add to the cost of the retailed product. The third stage is to tailor the marketing of olive oil to recognise a world where there are many cultures with food preferences which are different from the traditional olive oil producing countries. Stage three will bring the recognition that the people who use olive oil will change the world, and not the olive oil itself!

It is incumbent on the owners of olive groves to seck and acquire the knowledge and capacity to forge an industry which delivers prosperity to them, the 'ordinary people', not the corporations and institutions which exploit them.

Epilogue

Epilogue seems an appropriate term to cover the epidemic which has had, and will continue to have, an impact on the operational systems in the industry. Declared a pandemic, Covid-19 has affected the lives of many people, especially those living near each other in the cities.

In their effort to control the spread of the corona virus, governments enacted a range of restrictions aimed at separating individuals to limit transmission through proximity, wearing of face masks, restricted movement and interaction and closure of businesses.

The impact on the olive oil industry started at the farm where social distancing during harvesting and processing was introduced. This has necessitated the careful planning of shifts and all activities to accommodate the spatial and hygiene requirements of the health regulations which include cleaning, sanitation, disinfection, education programmes, monitoring of workers, testing and screening and management of those infected. All these adjustments have led to added costs of production and distribution.

Many producers worldwide rely on seasonal migrant labour to supplement local workers for harvesting and pruning. The travel restrictions and border closures have severely limited the movement of these workers forcing new approaches to labour hire. Local workers may be reluctant to go to work for fear of contracting the viral infection and the associated sickness and isolation. One inevitable consequence will be an acceleration of the move to mechanical harvesting to limit the risk of labour shortages in the future. Another approach may be the payment of higher wages to induce local unemployed to take on the harvesting work. In countries where unemployment benefits are paid, there may need to be an adjustment as a disincentive to continue a life of unemployment.

Labourers are not the only employees to be affected. With the northern and southern hemisphere production seasons allowing technicians to find work year-round, closed borders curtailed this. While these travelling technicians may be able to resume their six-monthly cycles in different hemispheres, it is likely that producers will train local employees to undertake the technical activities to reduce the risk of repeated limitations on international movement.

Further along the supply chain the traders have another layer of compliance to deal with – those relating to the sometimes-quirky requirements of different countries covering food handling and packaging in relation to the risk of spreading the virus. I use the term quirky as some of these requirements do not seem to be based on sound science which suggests that the spread of the virus through food preparation, consumption and related packaging is low risk.

Another impact on the supply side of olive oil is the restriction of movement of vehicles and increased handling costs for transport. This has led to delays in delivery and, for perishable products like olive oil, resulted in longer storage with the risk of oxidisation.

Consumer behaviour has changed either by choice with an aversion to interaction within others while shopping or at work, or by edict such as the lockdown measures introduced in most countries and the 'work from home' philosophy. The closure of many of the businesses in the Horeca sector forced people to stay home and cater and cook for themselves. Sales of olive oil to Horeca all but stopped while purchases by consumers through the supermarkets and groceries allowed to remain open have increased accordingly. Online purchases have also grown substantially. These changes to home cooking and shopping are likely to persist to some degree when restrictions are lifted as families rediscover the healthy meals with the entire family at home and the ease of shopping online. It is also apparent that consumers are more discerning in the quality of olive oil they purchase for home consumption, in some cases selecting a higher grade of vegetable oil than the cost conscious Horeca sector. This will have an impact on the balance of supply of olive pomace, refined olive oil and extra virgin olive oil.

The shift to healthier eating which has resulted from consumers eating out less, purchasing ingredients for home cooking and an increased need for knowledge of recipes and food preparation is an opportunity for the olive industry to expand and consolidate its position as the healthiest vegetable oil. This will require a change in the markets targeted by the promotional campaigns from foodservice to the more dispersed home cook. As restrictions are lifted the users who have been converted to olive oil during the pandemic must be retained and a strategy adopted to enlist them as advocates for use of all grades of olive oil in Horeca to replace other vegetable oils.

The changed attitude towards food purchase and use exhibited by consumers during lockdown must be studied and traditional promotional campaigns replaced with new campaigns based on the new habits. Some of these are greater attention to reducing food wastage, purchasing locally produced products to ensure food security, and eating healthier diets.

With the advent of vaccines for Covid-19 many of the measures introduced to limit its spread will slowly fall away. However, it is likely that human behaviour both in food purchasing, preparation and consumption will have changed permanently. The olive industry must identify these changes and adapt its marketing to take advantage of those which will increase the consumption of olive products.

The supply chain and consumers have been profoundly affected by Covid-19, as has been the service sector. The classification of olive oils by technical panels and the judging of competitions has become more dispersed with samples being distributed rather than panels converging. Time will tell whether the cost savings from this change result in permanent adjustments to these activities in the future. Another consequence for competitions may be that producers and distributors reduce the number of events entered as their online sales grow and their promotion shifts more towards social media with their websites as the foundation.

Education and training have been affected with many courses being converted to online presentation, others suspended, and some continuing with reduced numbers. It is likely that this sector will return to normal with the caveat that formats will recognise social distancing and a reluctance to travel will shrink the pool of potential participants. Unfortunately, this may lead to greater parochialism, the opposite of the cross-regional interaction and cooperation which is needed for unity of purpose in expanding consumption of olive oil.

Conferences and seminars will be similarly affected in the post-covid world. The move to online webinars may erode the place of in-person events. For a while there will be an aversion to large events with people coming from many countries. In time with immunisation and elimination of Coronavirus the international conference schedules for research exchange and discussion of industry issues will return. The future is likely to be a more balanced combination of online and in-person activities.

Trade fairs virtually ceased during the pandemic resulting in the organisers searching for alternatives. International surveys have been commissioned to gauge the mood of the exhibitors and attendees. Options canvassed include smaller regional events, rigorous infection testing regimes for everyone involved with associated deep cleaning and sanitisation. Whatever the formats adopted there will still be a diversity of limits on international travel and requirement for vaccination. The revamped events will be more costly, and exhibitors are likely to look for more cost-effective ways to promote their products. It will be some time before the trade fair circuit reaches its pre-covid levels of participation.

There is one other aspect of the pandemic which bears consideration. The spread of the virus is assisted by close living and the erosion of the disease prevention habits of personal hygiene. The impact of Coronavirus is less severe in rural areas where the population is more dispersed. Consider the rapid development of super high-density olive groves and the proximity of the trees to each other. This is a lack of horticultural social distancing which, if grove 'hygiene' is not maintained, could leave to the rapid spread of diseases such as Xylella fastidiosa. The ability of bacteria and viruses to mutate and develop resistance to bactericides and vaccines poses a constant threat to massive dense plant populations. Xylella fastidiosa, a threat to olives, almonds, cherries and plums, has been found in Italy, France, Spain and Portugal. If found in super high-density groves the consequences will be catastrophic.

The Covid-19 pandemic and the Xylella outbreak have restricted the movement of people and plant material respectively. Controls to combat both diseases have severely interrupted the normal flow of business in all regions involved in the production and consumption of olive products, especially olive oil. The global disruption has the potential to make people revert to parochialism as a defence against the perceived threat. This will cripple an industry which is already suffering from regional interests taking precedence over those which have industry-wide benefits. In politics it is easier to appeal to one's constituents than to take a more universal approach which elevates the entire industry. The diverse response to the Covid-19 pandemic from politicians has clearly demonstrated the easy return to a parochial message.

It will take great leadership to keep the global olive industry together with unity of purpose in the post-covid era. The 'ordinary people', those who work the groves and processing facilities and cannot work from home, are those most affected by the pandemic, economically and socially. Those at the IOC who profess to advance the well-being of the ordinary people are the least affected along with other bureaucrats and institutional employees who have been able to work from home with minimal impact, even increases, on their income.

For the sake of the 'ordinary people', the time has come for leaders of the entire industry to set aside their personal aspirations to concentrate on the onerous task of reshaping and reinvigorating the global olive industry in the post-covid era.

Glossary

AU$ - Australian dollar

AOOPA – American Olive Oil Producers Association

CSIRO – Commonwealth Scientific and Industrial Research Organisation (Australia)

DAGS – Diacylglycerols

EU – European Union

€ - Euro

FRF – Fruit removal force

FDA – Food and Drug Administration (USA)

GFC – Global Financial Crisis

Horeca – Hotel, restaurant, catering

IBC – Intermediate bulk container

IOC – International Olive Council

LSM – Living standards measure

MOAH – Mineral oil aromatic hydrocarbons

MOSH – Mineral oil saturated hydrocarbons

NAOOA - North American Olive Oil Association

NGO – Non-government organisation

NYIOOC – New York International Olive Oil Competition

ONAOO – Organizzazione Nazionale Assaggiatori Olio Di Oliva

PDO – Protected designation of origin

PGI – Protected geographical indication

PPP – Pyropheophytin

SKU – Stock-keeping unit

US$ - United States dollar

WIOO – Women in Olive Oil

WHO – World Health Organisation

Printed in Great Britain
by Amazon

37075329R00104